CHARLES F. STANLEY BIBLE STUDY SERIES

DISCOVERING YOUR IDENTITY

UNDERSTAND WHO YOU ARE
IN GOD'S EYES

CHARLES F. STANLEY

THOMAS NELSON
Since 1798

DISCOVERING YOUR IDENTITY
CHARLES F. STANLEY BIBLE STUDY SERIES

Copyright © 1996, 2008, 2020 by Charles F. Stanley.

Published in Nashville, Tennessee, by Thomas Nelson. Thomas Nelson is a registered trademark of HarperCollins Christian Publishing, Inc.

All Scripture quotations are taken from the New King James Version.® Copyright © 1982 by Thomas Nelson. Used by permission. All rights reserved worldwide.

Thomas Nelson titles may be purchased in bulk for educational, business, fundraising, or sales promotional use. For information, e-mail SpecialMarkets@ThomasNelson.com.

ISBN 978-0-310-10568-8 (softcover)
ISBN 978-0-310-10569-5 (ebook)

First Printing August 2020

CONTENTS

A Fresh Look at Your Identity as a Believer

We all have an outlook on the world and on life—a way of looking at things, valuing things, and judging things. This perspective is something we have *learned*. As a result, many of us today have a wrong understanding about certain things, such as our identity as believers in Christ. We truly do not know who we *are* in Christ. We have misconceptions about why God forgives, what salvation means to our life on this earth, and who God has called us to be.

In order to gain the right perspective, we need to go to the Word of God . . . and stay there. Books on self-esteem may be helpful, but only if they are firmly based on Scripture. The Bible is God's foremost communication on the subject of self-esteem and self-identity. We must return to it continually to discover who we are, how we are to respond to life's situations, and how we are to interact with others. Our perspective is wrong if it doesn't match up with God's truth.

This book can be used by you alone or by several people in a small-group study. At various times, you will be asked to relate to the material in one of the following four ways.

First, what new insights have you gained? Make notes about the insights you have. You may want to record them in your Bible or in a separate journal. As you reflect on your new understanding, you are likely to see how God has moved in your life.

Second, have you ever had a similar experience? You approach the Bible from your own unique background . . . your own particular set of understandings about the world that you bring with you when you open God's Word. For this reason, it is important to consider how your experiences are shaping your understanding and allow yourself to be open to the truth that God reveals.

Third, how do you feel about the material? While you should not depend solely on your emotions as a gauge for your faith, it is important for you to be aware of them as you study a passage of Scripture and can freely express them to God. Sometimes, the Holy Spirit will use your emotions to compel you to look at your life in a different or challenging way.

Fourth, in what way do you feel challenged to respond or to act? God's Word may inspire you or challenge you to take a particular action. Take this challenge seriously and find ways to move into it. If God reveals a particular need that He wants you to address, take that as His "marching orders." God will empower you to do something with the challenge that He has just given you.

Start your Bible study sessions in prayer. Ask God to give you spiritual eyes to see and spiritual ears to hear. As you conclude your study, ask the Lord to seal what you have learned so you will not forget it. Ask Him to help you grow into the fullness of the nature and character of Christ Jesus.

I encourage you to keep the Bible at the center of your study. A genuine Bible study stays focused on God's Word and promotes a growing faith and a closer walk with the Holy Spirit in each person who participates.

YOU ARE A SAINT!

IN THIS LESSON

Learning: What exactly is a saint?

Growing: How does "sainthood"
apply to my self-evaluation?

King David wrote, "Sing praise to the LORD, you *saints* of His, and give thanks at the remembrance of His holy name" (Psalm 30:4, emphasis added). Look at that word *saint* in this verse. Is this how you see yourself? Do you regard yourself as a saint?

Each of us acts on the basis of how we view ourselves. Our opinion of self directs and focuses our behavior every hour of every day. If we have a faulty self-image—which is having any self-image other than what God says about us—we will behave in a way that is contrary to God's highest purposes and plan for our lives. This is why having a correct self-image is important. It affects the way we make choices, deal with problems, and approach tasks and challenges in life. A correct self-image also impacts how we deal with other people.

Jesus taught that we are to love our neighbors *as we love ourselves*. He said to His disciples, "'You shall love the LORD your God with all your heart, with all your soul, and with all your mind.' This is the first and great commandment. And the second is like it: 'You shall love your neighbor as yourself.' On these two commandments hang all the Law and the Prophets" (Matthew 22:37–40). We are to love, appreciate, value, and treat others in the same way that we love, appreciate, value, and treat *ourselves*.

This means that if we do *not* love ourselves in an appropriate way, we cannot love others as God wants us to love them. A God-based self-image is vital if we are going to relate to others in a truly Christlike way. It is also vital if we want to show the love of God to them.

1. Why do you think that Jesus said loving your neighbor is like loving God? Why does He list loving God first before loving others?

....

....

....

....

....

2. Why do you think Jesus said, "love your neighbor as yourself," rather than, "learn to love yourself, then love your neighbor the same way"? Explain.

....

....

....

....

....

3. Why do "all the Law and the Prophets" hang from these two commandments?

....

....

....

....

....

....

....

THE BASIS FOR YOUR SAINTHOOD

The Bible says those who believe in Christ and have accepted Him as their Savior are *saints*—and each of us must choose to believe what the Bible says. This is not based on how we *feel*. Most of us do not feel like saints on any given day. But feelings come and go. What we feel is often highly unpredictable, and emotions are not a basis for making decisions about our true identity. For some people, an unruly hairdo or a spilled cup of coffee can ruin a day emotionally. No . . . emotions are not the basis on which we conclude that we are saints.

Nor is being a saint based on our *understanding* about sainthood. Few people can truly say they understand fully what it means to be a follower of Christ. None of us can fully explain the mystery of why God would choose to love us, forgive us, extend mercy and grace to us, or send His Son to die for us. A finite mind can never understand the infinite wisdom and power of almighty God. No . . . understanding is not the basis on which we conclude that we are saints.

Perhaps you have heard people say to you, "Oh, you are a real saint!" What they actually mean is, "You are truly a kind person, a generous person, or a helpful person." From a biblical point of view, sainthood has nothing to do with what we *do* in the form of good works or kind gestures. Sainthood is bestowed on those who believe in Christ solely on the basis of *what Jesus Christ has done*. The opinions of others are irrelevant and of no consequence.

So, what qualifies us to be saints? Only one thing: we must accept—receive, believe, and personally embrace—the sacrificial death of Jesus Christ on the cross. Our relationship with Jesus is what qualifies us to be saints. Nothing else is required!

However, within the concept of sainthood we find a number of other important truths. What does it truly *mean* to be a saint? How do saints live out their lives? What do saints do? These questions are at the heart of this study. When you acknowledge that you are a saint—a believer in Jesus Christ—you are just at the starting point for discovering *who you are in Christ*.

4. In what ways have you been relying on others to give you a sense of self-worth or to define your identity?

....

....

....

....

....

....

....

5. How do you feel about being called "a saint of God"? How do you generally think of yourself in that regard?

....

....

....

....

....

....

....

A "RIGHT" SELF-ESTEEM

We hear a great deal about self-esteem today. Countless books and online resources have been created on the subject. Nearly all of them are aimed at helping a person *raise* low self-esteem to achieve a *good* self-esteem. These resources address two broad categories.

First, there are some people who have self-esteem that is too *high*. In my opinion this represents a relatively small percentage of people, especially since many of those who *act* as if they think too highly of themselves are actually masking a low self-image. Those with too-high self-esteem are arrogant, self-centered, and have no regard for others. They believe the entire universe revolves around them. Too-high self-esteem leads them to conclude, "I can make it on my own if everybody else will just get out of my way." They suffer from the "Big I" syndrome.

Second, there are those who have self-esteem that is too *low*. Most people fall into this category. They look around and conclude, "I'm not good enough, capable enough, or valuable enough. I'm worthless." They see themselves without purpose or desirability. They cannot comprehend others might love them and value them—much less that *God* can love them.

In many cases, those with too-low self-esteem adopt a *false humility*—a kind of humility not before God but before others. They say, "I can't do what other people can do. I can't succeed as much as they succeed. I couldn't possibly be as effective as another person in this role." In their low self-esteem, they become "doormats" for others to walk on, which often leads to them feeling frustrated, discouraged, depressed, and without hope for their future.

What we don't tend to realize is that people with too-low self-esteem also see the world through the filter of their own self and their own lack of ability. They are just as guilty of the "Big I syndrome" as those with too-high self-esteem. They are focused too much on *themselves*.

6. "Let nothing be done through selfish ambition or conceit, but in lowliness of mind let each esteem others better than himself" (Philippians 2:3). Paul uses esteem as a verb in this verse. It is something you choose to do, not something that "just is." How does this apply to your own self-esteem?

....

....

....

....

....

7. What would your life be like if everyone you know esteemed themselves to be better than others? What if everyone esteemed others as better than themselves?

....

....

....

....

....

....

THE ERROR OF COMPARISON

One great error that people make, regardless of whether their self-esteem is too low or too high, is that they compare *themselves* to *others*. God never calls us to compare ourselves with anyone! Each of us has been given a unique, one-of-a kind, irreplaceable purpose in God's plan. We have been created *as we are* by a loving God who wants us to fulfill the purpose that *He* has for our lives. It is when we compare ourselves to others that we say, "I'm not like that person," and then conclude, "I'm not as good," or, "I'm so much better."

Comparison separates and divides us from one another. But of even greater consequence is the fact it leads us to false conclusions about ourselves and, therefore, to faulty behaviors. When we think we are better than others, we treat them as inferior or as failures. When we think we are not as valuable as others, we treat them with undue deference, resentment, and envy. Both sets of behaviors keep us from loving others completely or appreciating the fullness of *who* God made them to be.

God calls us to neither a too-high nor a too-low self-esteem. He wants us to have a *right* self-esteem. A correct self-image can never be rooted in comparison with others. It can never be concluded on the basis of what others think about us, say to us, or even the way we feel about ourselves. A correct self-image is based on what *God* says about us in His Word.

Correct self-esteem is opposite to the "Big I" syndrome. Correct self-esteem says we do not know ourselves fully—but God does. Correct self-esteem says we cannot determine our own goodness or achieve our own forgiveness and righteousness—but we can accept what Jesus has done on our behalf. Correct self-esteem concludes we do not have the ability to love others unconditionally in our own strength—but we can love others as God helps us love them.

What *God* says about our identity is opposite to what the world says. The world says, "You have to make your own success." God says, "Have a relationship with Me, trust Me, and I will give you total fulfillment and satisfaction." The world says, "If you don't make your own way, you will be run over or disregarded by others." God says, "The greatest among you will become the servant of all, and in that, I will be well pleased with you." The world says, "Get all you can so you can become all you are." God says, "Give away all you can so you can gain your own soul." God wants us to look to *Him* for our self-definition and our identity.

This is the focus of this study—*to who you are looking for your identity, image, and worth.* Perhaps you are listening to "replays" of what parents and others have said to you when you were a child. Some of those replays are faulty! Or maybe you are looking to spouses, family members, friends, bosses, teachers, or others in authority to define you. Recognize that in many cases their understanding of you is limited. Often, they don't know the real you at all! No other person in this world knows you fully nor has the ability to see your past or your future.

God is the only reliable source of accurate, wise, and eternal information about you. He alone loves you unconditionally, understands you fully, and knows the fullness of purpose that He has built into your life. If you are ever going to discover your *true* identity in Christ Jesus—if you are going to discover what it means to be a saint—you must turn to God and His Word.

8. In what ways have you been relying on others to give you a sense of your self-worth or to define your identity?

....

....

....

....

....

....

9. "Whoever desires to become great among you, let him be your servant. And whoever desires to be first among you, let him be your slave—just as the Son of Man did not come to be served, but to serve, and to give His life a ransom for many" (Matthew 20:26–28). What were Jesus' purposes in coming to earth? How do these purposes relate to your identity?

....

....

....

....

....

....

10. How do you react to the Lord's commandment to be a "slave"?

TODAY AND TOMORROW

Today: A too low self-esteem leads to the same errors
as a too high self-esteem: I become proud.

Tomorrow: I will ask the Lord to show me through
His Word how to have a right self-esteem.

CLOSING PRAYER

Father, we thank You for loving us. You are so patient to put up with our doubts, our fears, our anxieties, and so much of what has absolutely no basis whatsoever. Help us today to recognize the true identity that we have been given in Christ. Help us to see ourselves in the way that You see us—as Your chosen saints, ready and prepared to do Your work in this world.

Notes and Prayer Requests

• •

Use this space to write any key points, questions, or prayer requests from this week's study.

....

....

....

....

....

....

....

....

....

....

....

....

....

....

....

....

....

....

....

....

....

....

....

....

....

....

YOU ARE IN CHRIST

IN THIS LESSON

Learning: What does it mean to be "in Christ"?

Growing: How should my identity in Christ affect my view of myself?

Most Christians today do not seem to know who they are. If you ask them, "Who are you?" they are likely to respond with their name, where they work, to whom they are related, and so forth. One woman said to me, "I'm Jane . . . the wife of Tom, mother of Sally and Dennis, and daughter of George and Ruth." She went on to tell me the name of the company for which she worked. But when I asked her, "Okay, but who are you as a Christian?" she stared at me blankly and finally said, "Well, I'm a member of *your church*!"

I find this is a common response. Many people give the name of their denomination or their specific church when asked about their identity as a Christian. Some believe their identity as a Christian can be summed up by saying, "I'm baptized," or, "I'm a regular churchgoer," or, "I am a regular tither," or, "I've been saved for more than twenty-two years."

What you believe about yourself as a Christian determines your self-identity and your self-esteem. Your identity is not a matter of who you know, where you work, which neighborhood you live in, or who your friends are. Your identity as a believer flows from the relationship you have with God through Christ Jesus.

1. How do you tend to answer the question, "who are you"? Do you point to your roles or your position at work? How would you describe your identity as a follower of Christ?

2. "So God created man in His own image; in the image of God He created him; male and female He created them" (Genesis 1:27). What does it mean to be created in the "image" of God? How should that impact your own self-worth?

....

....

....

....

....

....

....

WHO YOU ARE IN CHRIST

It is critically important today for us to know who we are in Christ. The reason is because it is only when we know *who* we are that we can properly discern: (1) how we are to respond in any situation, (2) how we are to make decisions in the face of any problem or opportunity, (3) how we are to answer any question, (4) how we are to treat other people, (5) how we are to schedule our priorities in life, and (6) how we are to witness about Jesus Christ.

Our identity determines the way we feel about ourselves, our hopes for the future, and how we develop our talents and skills. In the Bible, we find the apostle Paul wrote about this subject of the true identity of a believer. His foremost conclusion about the believer's identity can be summed up in two words: "in Christ." For example, notice the number of times that he uses the phrase "in Christ" or "of Christ" in the following passage:

Paul, an apostle of Jesus Christ by the will of God, to the saints who are in Ephesus, and faithful in Christ Jesus:

Grace to you and peace from God our Father and the Lord Jesus Christ.

Blessed be the God and Father of our Lord Jesus Christ, who has blessed us with every spiritual blessing in the heavenly places in Christ, just as He chose us in Him before the foundation of the world, that we should be holy and without blame before Him in love, having predestined us to adoption as sons by Jesus Christ to Himself, according to the good pleasure of His will, to the praise of the glory of His grace, by which He made us accepted in the Beloved.

In Him we have redemption through His blood, the forgiveness of sins, according to the riches of His grace which He made to abound toward us in all wisdom and prudence, having made known to us the mystery of His will, according to His good pleasure which He purposed in Himself, that in the dispensation of the fullness of the times He might gather together in one all things in Christ, both which are in heaven and which are on earth—in Him.

In Him also we have obtained an inheritance, being predestined according to the purpose of Him who works all things according to the counsel of His will, that we who first trusted in Christ should be to the praise of His glory.

In Him you also trusted, after you heard the word of truth, the gospel of your salvation; in whom also, having believed, you were sealed with the Holy Spirit of promise, who is the guarantee of our inheritance until the redemption of the purchased possession, to the praise of His glory (Ephesians 1:1–14).

Our relationship with Christ is to be our inner motivation. It is to be our security and our confidence. Many of us today are drawing our identity from the label stitched on our clothing rather than drawing our identity from where our name is written: in the Lamb's Book of Life (see Revelation 13:8)! You are *in Christ*. So, if anyone asks you, "Who *are* you?" your answer should be this: "I am a believer in Christ Jesus. I am *in Christ*."

3. In the passage listed above, circle the phrases "in Christ," "in Him," "in Himself," "in the Beloved" (who is Christ), and "in whom" (when it refers to Christ) whenever they appear. What does it mean to be "in Christ"?

....

....

....

....

....

....

....

....

4. How does your being "in Christ" change the very definition of who you are?

....

....

....

....

....

....

....

....

YOUR OLD LIFE BEFORE CHRIST

Where were you before you were in Christ? The Bible says you were "in Adam." You were a natural heir of Adam, descended from the first man and woman created by God, who rebelled against God in their disobedience and became subject to sin and spiritual death. You were born naturally with a sinful state of heart. Your inclination was to sin, and your desire was to sin. Nobody ever teaches a little child to steal, lie, or to covet toys.

A child is born with a "me, myself, and I" complex. As Paul describes this state of being, "You He made alive, who were dead in trespasses and sins, in which you once walked according to the course of this world, according to the prince of the power of the air, the spirit who now works in the sons of disobedience, among whom also we all once conducted ourselves in the lusts of our flesh, fulfilling the desires of the flesh and of the mind, and were by nature children of wrath, just as the others" (Ephesians 2:1–3).

In your sinful state, you had no way to bring about your own forgiveness or freedom from sin and guilt. No person can earn forgiveness, because none of us have the authority to say to ourselves, "You are forgiven." A life "in Adam" is a life of darkness. You were blinded to the truth about God, separated from a relationship with God, and in bondage to sin's impulses—without genuine freedom to live a righteous life. It was a life headed for eternal death, which is the ultimate consequence of an unchanged sinful heart.

5. "But God, who is rich in mercy, because of His great love with which He loved us, even when we were dead in trespasses, made us alive together with Christ (by grace you have been saved), and raised us up together, and made us sit together in the heavenly places in Christ Jesus" (Ephesians 2:4–6). What does it mean to be "dead in trespasses"?

6. If you were once dead, but have now been made alive again, what does this suggest about your identity "in Christ"?

....

....

....

....

....

....

....

....

....

....

....

YOUR NEW LIFE IN CHRIST

Throughout Paul's epistle to the Ephesians, he gives a vivid and complete description of your life "in Adam." But he does not end the story there. Paul goes on to give the hope and great contrast of your life now as a believer—a life *in Christ*. As he writes, "Now in Christ Jesus you who once were far off have been brought near by the blood of Christ" (Ephesians 2:13).

The life you have in Christ is made possible at God's initiative and by Jesus' death on the cross. God was motivated by His love to save humankind, so He did for us what we could not do for ourselves— He completely and eternally bridged the gap created by our sin so *all* who believe in Christ Jesus might be forgiven and have eternal life.

As John wrote, "For God so loved the world that He gave His only begotten Son, that whoever believes in Him should not perish but have everlasting life. For God did not send His Son into the world to condemn the world, but that the world through Him might be saved. He who believes in Him is not condemned; but he who does not believe is condemned already, because he has not believed in the name of the only begotten Son of God" (John 3:16–18).

Believing and accepting the work that Jesus did on the cross is *all* that is required for you to exchange your old identity "in Adam" to your new identity "in Christ." In fact, it is *the* requirement. No substitution for this requirement will work—no amount of good works, no amount of self-help techniques, no amount of thinking good thoughts or striving to be a good person. The apostle Paul made it clear: "For by grace you have been saved through faith, and that not of yourselves; it is the gift of God, not of works, lest anyone should boast" (Ephesians 2:8–9).

7. "For since by man came death, by Man also came the resurrection of the dead. For as in Adam all die, even so in Christ all shall be made alive" (1 Corinthians 15:21–22). Make a list of all the things that you inherited from Adam. In a parallel column, make a list of all that you inherited from Christ.

8. Referring to the list in the last question, how would you define yourself when you were "in Adam"? How would you define yourself now "in Christ"?

_____

_____

_____

_____

_____

_____

_____

_____

_____

_____

_____

_____

_____

_____

How to Live in Christ

Throughout the New Testament, we find a number of descriptions about what it means to be made alive "in Christ." As Paul writes in 2 Corinthians 5:17–18, "Therefore, if anyone is in Christ, he is a new creation; old things have passed away; behold, all things have become new. Now all things are of God, who has reconciled us to Himself through Jesus Christ."

Once we are in Christ, we are not to draw from a deposit of previous good works. We are not to believe the "old lies" playing in our heads since early childhood that we are worthless, unwanted, or undesirable. We are new creatures with a new life ahead—a life that is reconciled to God and is set on a path toward fulfillment and satisfaction in Christ Jesus.

Jesus described this life as a branch abiding in a vine. "I am the vine, you are the branches. He who abides in Me, and I in him, bears much fruit; for without Me you can do nothing. If anyone does not abide in Me, he is cast out as a branch and is withered; and they gather them and throw them into the fire, and they are burned. If you abide in Me, and My words abide in you, you will ask what you desire, and it shall be done for you. By this My Father is glorified, that you bear much fruit; so you will be My disciples" (John 15:5–8).

When we are in Christ, we have a heart bent toward God. We are able to receive and enjoy those things the Lord has reserved exclusively for us as believers. We are empowered to lead a godly life. We pursue a life marked by the fruit of the Holy Spirit and a bold witness for Christ. What freedom! We are not destined to receive what we deserved when we were "in Adam." No more striving, climbing the ladder of acceptability, or performing in hopes of gaining God's applause. Our new life in Christ is not based on what we do but on who we *are* in Christ.

9. In what ways does a branch depend on the trunk for survival and nourishment? Give some practical ways in which you are called to do the same in Christ.

10. "Therefore, if anyone is in Christ, he is a new creation; old things have passed away; behold, all things have become new" (2 Corinthians 5:17). What "old things" have passed away from your identity before becoming a Christian? What things have "become new" in your identity?

....

....

....

....

TODAY AND TOMORROW

Today: My true identity comes entirely through the grace and sacrifice of Jesus Christ.

Tomorrow: I will prayerfully study the Word of God this week to learn what it means to be "in Christ."

CLOSING PRAYER

Lord, thank You for the promise that we are "in Christ." In light of who we are, by the gift of Your grace, we pray that we will walk in a manner worthy of our place. We praise You for the identity You have given to us. We praise You that this identity is not based on what we have, where we live, what we drive, where we have attended school, or our position and prominence in the world—but completely on the basis of Jesus residing within us as our living Lord.

Notes and Prayer Requests

. . . .

Use this space to write any key points, questions, or prayer requests from this week's study.

YOU ARE CHOSEN BY GOD

IN THIS LESSON

Learning: What does it mean to be "chosen by God"?

Growing: If I have been adopted by God, how should that affect my life?

Are you aware that as a believer in Christ Jesus, you have been *chosen* by God? What a wonderful word that is! *Chosen* speaks of value, worthiness, love, and appreciation. To be chosen means that others *want* to be with us, *want* to know us, *want* to spend time with us. Certainly, all of those things are true when it comes to God's choosing to be reconciled to us in Christ Jesus and choosing us as His children. In selecting us, God is saying, "I want to be in a close relationship with you. I want to spend time with you. I want to share Myself with you."

As a believer in Jesus, you are a saint in Christ *and* you have been chosen by God to have a special relationship with Him. As the apostle Paul wrote, "Blessed be the God and Father of our Lord Jesus Christ, who has blessed us with every spiritual blessing in the heavenly places in Christ, just as *He chose us in Him before the foundation of the world*, that we should be holy and without blame before Him in love" (Ephesians 1:3–4, *emphasis added*).

1. When have you felt "chosen" for something special? How did you respond?

2. What does it mean to you to know that you have been personally chosen by God?

God Does the Choosing

As we study what it means to be chosen by God, we must be certain about one thing: *it is God who does the choosing.* As Paul wrote to the believers in Ephesus, "He chose us in Him before the foundation of the world" (Ephesians 1:4). In other words, from the very beginning of all things, God *planned* to be in relationship with you through Christ Jesus. You were always a part of God's plan and purpose. You were always chosen by God—even before you personally accepted Jesus as your Savior.

You have always been a *desired child* of God. So many children grow up being told by their parents, "We never really wanted you. You were an accident. You were a surprise." The truth from God's perspective is something entirely different: God *always* wanted you. You were part of His design and His plan from the foundation of the earth. You were intended, expected, and created by God for precisely this time and for a precise purpose.

God didn't say when you were born, "Well, what can I do about this child?" No! God said at your birth, "This is the child whom I created for this specific time, place, and purpose on the earth!" Furthermore, Paul wrote that God chose us "according to the good pleasure of His will" (verse 5). In other words, God created you because it *pleased* Him to create you.

None of us can fathom God's grace in choosing us. Nothing that you ever did or could do put you into a position to be chosen by God. You didn't say the right things, do the right things, or become the right person. God chose you simply because He *wanted* to choose you and because He *desired* to be in relationship with you. He made a sovereign choice, completely based on His own motivation of love and on His abundant mercy.

Grace is the undeserved favor of God. You are the recipient of that divine grace. Your being chosen is the act of a loving God who chose you solely because He wanted to do so.

3. "You are a chosen generation, a royal priesthood, a holy nation, His own special people, that you may proclaim the praises of Him who called you out of darkness into His marvelous light" (1 Peter 2:9). How would you define the terms chosen generation, royal priesthood, and holy nation?

....

....

....

....

....

....

....

....

....

....

....

4. According to this verse, for what purpose has God chosen you? How does this influence your perspective about yourself?

....

....

....

....

....

....

....

....

....

....

....

....

PREDESTINED TO BE ADOPTED

Paul conveyed the truth of our being chosen by using two key terms: *predestined* and *adopted*. He says about God, "He chose us in Him [Christ] before the foundation of the world . . . having predestined us to adoption as sons by Jesus Christ to Himself" (Ephesians 1:4–5). Does God make choices? Yes! God *chose* the nation of Israel: "My people, My chosen. This people I have formed for Myself; they shall declare My praise" (Isaiah 43:20–21). God *chose* Jesus to be the Lamb slain from the foundation of the world (Revelation 13:8). God *chose* you to be His person on the earth today.

Many Christians are divided on the issue of predestination. There are those who put the emphasis on *our choice* to receive God's love and forgiveness. There are those who put the emphasis on *God's will* to choose a person by pouring out His love and forgiveness as He desires. The fact is that both viewpoints are correct! The invitation to receive God's forgiveness is extended to all . . . and the net result is that some are chosen.

Paul spoke clearly to the Ephesians about being predestined. Yet he also had this to say to the Romans about the Hebrew people, who saw themselves as the chosen people of God:

> I could wish that I myself were accursed from Christ for my brethren, my countrymen according to the flesh, who are Israelites, to whom pertain the adoption, the glory, the covenants, the giving of the law, the service of God, and the promises; of whom are the fathers and from whom, according to the flesh, Christ came, who is over all, the eternally blessed God. Amen.
>
> But it is not that the word of God has taken no effect. For they are not all Israel who are of Israel, nor are they all children because they are the seed of Abraham . . . Why? Because they did not seek it by faith, but as it were, by the works of the

law. . . . Brethren, my heart's desire and prayer to God for
Israel is that they may be saved (Romans 9:3–7, 32; 10:1).

Paul was the first to say that not all of Israel, the "chosen people,"
were predestined to salvation. He concluded, "Whoever calls on the
name of the LORD shall be saved" (10:13). Paul invested his life
in preaching the gospel to *all*. As he said to the Corinthians, "For
though I am free from all men, I have made myself a servant to all,
that I might win the more. . . . I have become all things to all men, that
I might by all means save some. Now this I do for the gospel's sake,
that I may be partaker of it with you" (1 Corinthians 9:19, 22–23).

No person can ever fully understand the concept of humankind's free will and God's predestined choice. It is a matter of faith—
accepting God's Word as truth and recognizing that we have been
chosen by God to be saints in Christ. Prior to our salvation and our
acceptance of Christ, each of us fell into the "loved-yet-perishing"
category (see John 3:16). After we accept Christ, we find ourselves
in the "predestined to adoption" category (see Ephesians 1:5).

So, do not focus on what might have been if you had not received
God's forgiveness and accepted Jesus Christ as your Savior. Instead,
put your focus on who you are as a believer. You are a chosen saint
of God . . . and were chosen from the foundation of the world!

5. How do you respond to the idea that God personally chose you
to receive salvation?

6. "The Lord is not slack concerning His promise, as some count slackness, but is longsuffering toward us, not willing that any should perish but that all should come to repentance" (2 Peter 3:9). What does this say about God's desire for all people to come to Christ? What does this say about His choice in who will be saved?

....

....

....

....

....

....

....

....

....

....

Your Rights Through Adoption

Paul further wrote that we were predestined for a specific role: to be *adopted children* of God (see Ephesians 1:5). Now, adoption in Paul's day was a little different than it is today. For instance, a father in Rome could disown a natural-born child, but he could not legally disown an adopted child. Adopted children had full rights to all that a father left as an inheritance and to the full use of the father's name. Adoption was highly prized in Rome because it carried with it great legal privileges and societal recognition.

In a culture in which natural-born children were often overlooked, discarded, or shut out of a father's presence, adopted children were conveyed the full rights of "sonship." Paul's goal in writing to the Ephesians was for them to understand this was their position in Christ. God had chosen them to be *sons*. They were in a privileged position before God!

7. "But when the fullness of the time had come, God sent forth His Son, born of a woman, born under the law, to redeem those who were under the law, that we might receive the adoption as sons. . . . Therefore you are no longer a slave but a son, and if a son, then an heir of God through Christ" (Galatians 4:4–5, 7). How would you describe some of the differences between being a slave and being a son?

....

....

....

....

....

....

....

....

....

....

8. How does the fact you are adopted into God's family change your view of yourself?

....

....

....

....

....

....

....

....

....

....

....

....

NO CAUSE FOR BOASTING

So, you are a chosen saint of God, predestined from the foundation of the world as an adopted child of God. What an awesome identity you have as a believer in Christ! But is this cause for boasting? Is your identity a reason to separate yourself from other people or to think of yourself more highly than those who are still "in Adam"? The Bible offers a resounding *no*!

Rather, your identity in Christ as a chosen and adopted child should give you *more compassion* for those who are outside of Christ. You should be more compelled to share the message of the gospel so that others might be among the "whoever believes" group. Knowing the great privilege it is to be a chosen child of God should compel you to bring others into fellowship with you, so that they might also be joint heirs with Christ of all things and the recipient of all spiritual blessings!

God hates pride wherever He finds it. As we read in Proverbs, "These six things the LORD hates, yes, seven are an abomination to Him: a proud look, a lying tongue, hands that shed innocent blood, a heart that devises wicked plans, feet that are swift in running to evil, a false witness who speaks lies, and one who sows discord among brethren" (6:16–19).

Pride will have no place in heaven. So, we are wise to come humbly before God with praise and thanksgiving for choosing us, and say to Him, "Abba, Father, thank You for choosing me to be Your child." It is as we recognize we are chosen that we then must choose to serve, choose to witness, and choose to praise God with every breath that we take.

9. "You did not receive the spirit of bondage again to fear, but you received the Spirit of adoption by whom we cry out, "Abba, Father" (Romans 8:15). The word Abba means "daddy" in Hebrew. Have you ever called God "Daddy" when praying? If so,

how does that intimacy affect your view of yourself and your relationship with God?

....
....
....
....
....
....
....
....

10. What is the "spirit of bondage to fear"? How does fear influence your view of yourself? How does your adoption by God influence that fear?

....
....
....
....
....
....
....
....

TODAY AND TOMORROW

Today: I have been both called and chosen by God Himself— and that alone makes me valuable.

Tomorrow: I will spend time in worship and thanksgiving this week, praising God for adopting me.

CLOSING PRAYER

. . . .

Father, thank You for Your goodness and mercy. Sovereign God of this universe, nothing is beyond Your knowledge or beyond Your reach. We humble ourselves before You today and thank You for choosing us. Our motivation is not to sit idle but to share the gospel of Christ with everyone we meet. By Your grace, we pray that You will reach out to us when we are feeling insignificant or unworthy so we can hear You say that we are accepted in the Beloved.

NOTES AND PRAYER REQUESTS

Use this space to write any key points, questions, or prayer requests from this week's study.

You Are a Beloved Child

IN THIS LESSON

Learning: Why does God love me?

Growing: How does God's love influence my identity?

You are not only God's adopted child, but you are God's *beloved* child. As the apostle Paul wrote, "Therefore, as the elect of God, holy and *beloved*, put on tender mercies, kindness, humility, meekness, long-suffering; bearing with one another, and forgiving one another, if anyone has a complaint against another; even as Christ forgave you, so you also must do" (Colossians 3:12–13). You are both *holy* and *beloved* by God.

Your heavenly Father's love for you is unconditional and unlimited. Many people have a difficult time accepting this idea of God's love. Others may accept the idea but place conditions on it. However, it is important for us to acknowledge God's unconditional love as part of our spiritual identity. This is because the degree to which we *receive* unconditional love is directly linked to the degree that we are able to *give* unconditional love to others.

Do you put qualifiers on God's love? Do you find yourself objecting to the fact that God loves you? Do you have a hard time in truly believing that God could love you in spite of your past? If so, you are rejecting a part of your spiritual identity as a believer—the fact that you *are* the beloved child of God. Paul wrote that we are "accepted in the Beloved" (Ephesians 1:6). The "Beloved," of course, is Christ Jesus. Few would argue that God the Father loved Jesus. After all, it is inconceivable to think a loving God would not love the Son—a member of the holy Trinity!

As believers, we are "in Christ." Our entire identity before God the Father is clothed in the righteousness and identity of Jesus Christ. We are part of the Beloved. We are loved because we are in Christ Jesus . . . and God loves Jesus.

1. How do you feel when you hear the words, "God loves you"? Do you ever put conditions on God's love for you? What areas in your life are dictated by a need to earn His love?

....

....

....

....

....

....

....

....

2. "In this the love of God was manifested toward us, that God has sent His only begotten Son into the world, that we might live through Him. In this is love, not that we loved God, but that He loved us and sent His Son to be the propitiation for our sins" (1 John 4:9–10). According to these verses, how much does God love you? What have you done to win God's love? What can you do in the future to retain His love?

....

....

....

....

....

....

....

....

....

....

....

....

God's Love Is Everlasting

God *initiates* love. He does not react to love. He loves *first*. John wrote, "We love Him because He first loved us" (1 John 4:19). Paul noted, "When the kindness and the love of God our Savior toward man appeared, not by works of righteousness which we have done, but according to His mercy He saved us, through the washing of regeneration and renewing of the Holy Spirit, whom He poured out on us abundantly through Jesus Christ our Savior" (Titus 3:4–6).

We didn't *earn* the coming of Jesus. We didn't *deserve* the death of God's Son on the cross. We didn't *qualify* ourselves to be recipients of God's kindness, love, or mercy. God *chose* to love us—and He continues to choose to love us. As He said through the prophet Jeremiah, "Yes, I have loved you with an everlasting love" (Jeremiah 31:3).

The good news about God's love is there is nothing that we can do to make God "un-love" us. So many Christians seem to think that when they sin or fall short of God's plan, they disappoint God, and He ceases to love them. No! The fact is that there is nothing we have ever done to deserve God's love. No amount of good works, kindness, perfected personality, or charitable deeds can win God's love. God chooses to love, and the motivation rests entirely in Him. He loves because He is loving.

John put is plainly when he wrote, "God is love" (1 John 4:8). It is God's *nature* to love, and His nature does not change according to our human behavior. There is nothing that we have done or ever could do to earn God's love—and there is nothing that we can ever do to stop God from loving us. Not even for a moment. His love for us is *everlasting*.

3. When have you loved another person unconditionally, even though that person may not have seemed "worthy" of love? Who has done that for you?

4. "For God so loved the world that He gave His only begotten Son, that whoever believes in Him should not perish but have everlasting life" (John 3:16). What does this suggest about God's love for you personally? What does it suggest about your true identity?

....

....

....

....

....

....

....

....

....

....

....

....

....

GOD LOVES WHAT GOD CREATES

When God created you, He loved you. Stated another way, God does not create what God does not love. Everything that God created was declared to be "good"—perfect, whole, valuable, lovable. God does not make junk. He doesn't make messes. God creates what He considers to be worthy of His love, His tender care, and His eternal presence.

Furthermore, God does not pour out His Spirit on what He does not love. When you accepted Jesus Christ as your Savior, God immediately moved into your life through the power of the Holy Spirit. God does not reside in a vessel that He does not love.

As Paul writes, "For by grace you have been saved through faith, and that not of yourselves; it is the gift of God, not of works, lest anyone should boast" (Ephesians 2:8–9). God is in the process of making you, fulfilling you, and bringing you to the full purpose of your life.

He is transforming you into the likeness of Jesus Christ. And He is doing so with tender and infinite love for you. He is fashioning you, molding you, chiseling you to be the beloved child with whom He desires to live forever. God loves what God makes—including *you!*

There is nothing you can do to cause God to stop loving you. There is nothing anyone else can do to keep God from loving you. As a believer in Christ Jesus, no outside force can cause God to stop loving you. Paul was clear on this point when he wrote: "Who shall separate us from the love of Christ? Shall tribulation, or distress, or persecution, or famine, or nakedness, or peril, or sword? . . . I am persuaded that neither death nor life, nor angels nor principalities nor powers, nor things present nor things to come, nor height nor depth, nor any other created thing, shall be able to separate us from the love of God" (Romans 8:35, 38–39).

5. "Hope does not disappoint, because the love of God has been poured out in our hearts by the Holy Spirit who was given to us" (Romans 5:5). When are times in your life that God's hope encouraged you or kept you going?

6. Look through Paul's list of everything that cannot separate you from God's love. What types of entities does he name? What does this say about the power of God's love?

....

....

....

....

....

....

....

....

....

....

....

....

....

YOUR RESPONSE TO GOD'S LOVE

As a follower of Christ, there are three responses you need to make to God's gift of love. *First, acknowledge it and accept it.* My prayer for you is the prayer that Paul prayed for the Thessalonians: "Now may the Lord direct your hearts into the love of God" (2 Thessalonians 3:5). Receive God's love. Open your heart and pray, "Lord, I know You love me according to the truth of Your Word. Help me to receive Your love so I feel Your loving presence always."

Second, live in God's love. As we stated, God's love is part of His nature. His love is *always* flowing out toward you. As Jude wrote, "Keep yourselves in the love of God, looking for the mercy of our Lord Jesus Christ unto eternal life" (Jude 21). John wrote that "God is love, and he who abides in love abides in God, and God in him" (1 John 4:16). Nurture your understanding of God's love and seek to dwell in that love daily. Thank the Lord each morning for His love. Remind yourself often, "God loves me!"

Third, love others. As you fully receive and abide in God's love, you are to be a vessel of that love, poured out to others. Loving others is not just a nice idea but a commandment of God. Jesus said, "This is My commandment, that you love one another as I have loved you. Greater love has no one than this, than to lay down one's life for his friends" (John 15:12–13).

7. How has Jesus loved you? Give examples both from Scripture and your own life.

....

....

....

....

....

....

....

....

....

....

....

8. According to Jesus' words, how are you called to love others? How does this calling affect your identity?

....

....

....

....

....

....

....

....

....

....

EXPERIENCE MORE OF GOD'S LOVE

Those who abide in God's love and express His love to others will experience even *more* of God's love. This does not mean God loves them more—as we have said, God's love is infinite and eternal at all times. Rather, it means those who abide in God's love, and who express that love, *experience* that love in increasingly more profound and joyful ways.

As Paul wrote, "I bow my knees to the Father . . . that Christ may dwell in your hearts through faith; that you, being rooted and grounded in love, may be able to comprehend with all the saints what is the width and length and depth and height—to know the love of Christ which passes knowledge; that you may be filled with all the fullness of God" (Ephesians 3:14, 17–19).

If you desire to *feel* more of God's love and to grow in your relationship with God, *receive* God's love by faith, choose to *abide* in God's love daily, and *show* God's love to others. What you give of God's love will be what you receive back—in multiplied form!

9. "If someone says, 'I love God,' and hates his brother, he is a liar; for he who does not love his brother whom he has seen, how can he love God whom he has not seen?" (1 John 4:20). Think about one or two people that you have trouble loving. What will you do this week to better show them God's love?

....

....

....

....

....

....

....

....

10. "Be of one mind, having compassion for one another; love as brothers, be tenderhearted, be courteous; not returning evil for evil or reviling for reviling, but on the contrary blessing, knowing that you were called to this, that you may inherit a blessing" (1 Peter 3:8–9). What are some ways that you can practice loving others in this way? What is the promise of what you will receive when you do this?

....

....

....

....

....

....

....

....

....

....

....

....

....

....

TODAY AND TOMORROW

Today: Nothing can ever separate me from God's love—nothing in heaven, earth, or hell!

Tomorrow: I will make a deliberate effort to show God's love to others, loving them as I love myself.

CLOSING PRAYER

. . . .

Lord, we thank You that Jesus gave us such a beautiful example to follow. He looked on the woman taken in adultery and saw her in all of her sin, forgave her, and told her to go and sin no more. He looked on the rich young ruler, loved him, and challenged him to lay aside his worldly wealth and follow after Him. Wherever we see Jesus, we see Him loving sacrificially—reaching out, forgiving, and serving those in need. He revealed to the people of His day—and to us—that we are accepted in God and are His beloved children. May we follow the example of Jesus today.

NOTES AND
PRAYER REQUESTS

Use this space to write any key points, questions, or prayer requests from this week's study.

You Are Redeemed

IN THIS LESSON

Learning: What difference does it make
that my sins are forgiven?

Growing: How does my salvation affect my identity?

Are you living today knowing fully that you are redeemed? Do you have the identity of a person who has been freed of sin's bondage? Do you feel fully and forever forgiven?

Many Christians today *say* they have been forgiven of all their sins, but they often do so with a small question mark in their voices—as if they are *hoping* they are forgiven rather than *knowing with certainty* that they are forgiven. Others believe their sins have been forgiven, but they continue to struggle with sin. They wonder if their ongoing struggle means they were not fully forgiven. They question whether they can ever be free of sinful desires and sinful habits.

Paul wrote this wonderful statement about our identity as believers in Ephesians 1:7: "In Him we have redemption through His blood, the forgiveness of sins, according to the riches of His grace." In this lesson, we will deal with our true identity as those who have been "redeemed by the blood of Christ Jesus."

1. When have you wondered whether God had truly forgiven you of your sin nature? When have you struggled with an ongoing desire to sin?

....

....

....

....

....

....

....

....

....

....

2. According to Ephesians 1:7, how can you know that God has fully forgiven you? What does His forgiveness depend on?

....

....

....

....

....

....

....

....

....

....

YOUR BEFORE AND AFTER STATE

Paul uses two words to describe the believer's relationship to sin: *redemption* and *forgiveness*. To be *forgiven* is to be set free from any guilt over past sins. It is to have the "sin slate" totally wiped clean. Sin is regarded throughout the Bible as a state of bondage resulting from transgressions and evil. We commit sin because we *are* sinners. We were born with a sin nature. Our sinful actions further seal the fact that we are sinners.

All sinners know they are sinning. Sin involves the will, and it involves our memory. We remember our sins. They don't just float by unnoticed or ignored. King David acknowledged this truth when he wrote, "For I acknowledge my transgressions, and my sin is always before me" (Psalm 51:3). Each of us is born with a sin nature, each of us commits sin, and each of us is in need of forgiveness. There is no person, aside from Christ, who was naturally good or without sin. Every person is in need of God's salvation to avoid the consequences of sin.

Our state prior to receiving God's forgiveness is that *we were living in sin*—the end result of which is *eternal death*. God's nature is holiness and truth, so He cannot abide where evil is allowed to reign. God always loves the sinner. But He is never content to allow sinners to continue in sin, because as long as they continue in sin, they are just beyond the reach of God's forgiveness. God is always working to bring sinners to the forgiveness offered through Jesus Christ so He can cause a spiritual rebirth in those individuals and abide with them.

Our state after receiving God's forgiveness is this: *we are living in the righteousness of Jesus Christ*—the end result of which is *eternal life*. By the power of His Holy Spirit, God abides within us and lives His life through us. Every believer is thus a walking picture of "before and after." Before Christ, we were unforgiven and were on a path to eternal death. But now, in Christ, we are forgiven and are on a path toward eternal life.

3. "For all have sinned and fall short of the glory of God" (Romans 3:23). What does it mean to "fall short" of the glory of God? What part does sin play in your self-identity?

....

....

....

....

....

....

4. "You He made alive, who were dead in trespasses and sins" (Ephesians 2:1). According to this verse, how did you become alive again? How does this influence your identity?

....

....

....

....

....

....

GOD'S FORGIVENESS IS TOTAL

Many people think their slate of sins has been only *partially* wiped clean. They look at the seriousness of their sin and wonder, "Could God ever fully forgive *that type of sin*?" Others look at the great number of their sins and question, "Could God ever fully forgive *so much sin?*" Still others look at the magnitude of a particular sin and ask, "Could God ever fully forgive *such a great sin*?" The answer to each question is an unqualified yes!

In the first place, God does not place qualifiers on sin. In His eyes, no one type of sin is any greater or lesser, blacker or darker, than any other kind of sin. Before God, sin is sin. Neither does God look at the amount of sin in a person's life and declare that—with the addition of one more sin—a person moves from the "forgivable" to the "unforgivable" column. All sin, no matter the amount, is equal before God. One sin is the same as one million sins. One type of sin is just as serious as any other.

When God forgives sin, He forgives it completely, even to the point of *forgetting it entirely*! As the writer of Hebrews states, "For this is the covenant that I will make with the house of Israel after those days, says the LORD: I will put My laws in their mind and write them on their hearts; and I will be their God, and they shall be My people. None of them shall teach his neighbor, and none his brother, saying, 'Know the Lord,' for all shall know Me, from the least of them to the greatest of them. For I will be merciful to their unrighteousness, and their sins and their lawless deeds I will remember no more" (Hebrews 8:10–12).

Not one shred of sin is left over for later forgiveness. God's ability to forgive sin is infinite and inexhaustible.

5. "You have lovingly delivered my soul from the pit of corruption, for You have cast all my sins behind Your back" (Isaiah 38:17). Which of your sins has God "cast behind His back"? What does this say about God's ability to forgive you for those sins?

6. "As far as the east is from the west, so far has He removed our transgressions from us" (Psalm 103:12). If you travel around the globe heading east, at what point will you begin heading west? What does this imply about God's forgiveness of your sins?

....

....

....

....

....

....

....

....

....

....

....

....

No One Is Turned Away

One awe-inspiring aspect of God's character is that He is merciful and forgiving to all who seek His forgiveness. All who ask God for forgiveness are granted it. Jesus said, "The one who comes to Me I will by no means cast out" (John 6:37). Our part is to come to God with a humble heart, confess we have sinned and are in need of forgiveness, accept Jesus Christ's sacrifice, and receive the forgiveness that God offers. God's response to our confession is always to forgive.

There simply is no basis for *refusing* to accept God's forgiveness. It is freely offered to all, it costs us nothing to receive, and it results in the guaranteed benefits of freedom from guilt and eternal life! God offers to forgive us completely. Once we repent of those sins, we must then let go of the guilt of the past. After all, if we hang on to guilt after receiving God's forgiveness, we are saying to God,

"Your forgiveness wasn't enough." And surely it is! The challenge for many of us is to *accept* God's total forgiveness and then to *forgive ourselves* and move forward in our lives. To hang on to guilt and shame is to devalue what Christ Jesus did on the cross.

Furthermore, not only are we forgiven, but we have also been redeemed from sin's bondage. To be *redeemed* is to be "delivered by payment of debt." Redemption is the *purchase* of something that has a debt against it. We see this in the way pawnshops are operated: those who buy things are buying items that have a debt against them. As we discussed earlier in this lesson, sinners carry a "debt" of sin. In their sinful state, they are living under a death sentence.

When Jesus died on the cross, He paid our sin debt and purchased us for God. Paul compared this purchase to the slave markets of the Roman Empire. He wrote, "Do you not know that to whom you present yourselves slaves to obey, you are that one's slaves whom you obey, whether of sin leading to death, or of obedience leading to righteousness? But God be thanked that though you were slaves of sin, yet you obeyed from the heart . . . And having been set free from sin, you became slaves of righteousness . . . Now having been set free from sin, and having become slaves of God, you have your fruit to holiness, and the end, everlasting life" (Romans 6:16–18, 22).

Slaves do what they are compelled to do by their masters. Paul stated that those who are still in a sinful state are slaves to their sin nature. They behave as they do because their sin nature compels them to do what is unrighteous in God's eyes. However, those who have received God's forgiveness have the Holy Spirit dwelling within them. They are compelled to act in a righteous way because of His presence in their lives.

Only a free person can buy a slave—and the only truly "free" person who ever walked this earth was Christ Jesus. He was the only One capable of purchasing us from the "slave market" of sin. By His shed blood, He made it possible for us to be forgiven and redeemed *so that we no longer have a sin nature and we no longer are slaves to sin.*

This means that as believers, we do not *have* to sin. The Holy Spirit dwelling in us will do His utmost to keep us from sinning, and if we sin, He will convict us so we will confess our sin and repent of it. Sinning is no longer our natural impulse. It has become unnatural and abhorrent to us. Our redemption means we are now in the process of losing all desire to sin.

As John writes, "If anyone sins, we have an Advocate with the Father. . . . Now by this we know that we know Him, if we keep His commandments. He who says, 'I know Him,' and does not keep His commandments, is a liar, and the truth is not in him. But whoever keeps His word, truly the love of God is perfected in him. By this we know that we are in Him. He who says he abides in Him ought himself also to walk just as He walked" (1 John 2:1, 3–6).

7. "Repent therefore and be converted, that your sins may be blotted out, so that times of refreshing may come from the presence of the Lord" (Acts 3:19). What does it mean to have your "sins blotted out"? If ink is erased, how can it be "un-erased"?

8. Even though a son cannot be forced back into slavery, he might still choose to act like a slave. When has this been true in your own life?

....

....

....

....

....

....

....

....

LIVING AS THOSE WHO HAVE BEEN REDEEMED

Many people question the security of salvation, falsely believing Christians can be saved and then live any way they choose without consequence. There is always consequence to sin! Believers in Christ Jesus will not lose their salvation and eternal life if they choose to sin. But they will set themselves up for a lifetime of misery if they sin in the face of God's loving forgiveness. The Holy Spirit acts within each of us to convict us of sin and to draw us back to the throne of God—to confess that sin and receive forgiveness for it.

Those who pursue a life of sin have probably not been born again. John writes, "By this we know that we love the children of God, when we love God and keep His commandments. For this is the love of God, that we keep His commandments. And His commandments are not burdensome. For whatever is born of God overcomes the world. And this is the victory that has overcome the world—our faith" (1 John 5:2–4).

Those who have been redeemed and forgiven of their sins will no longer have a desire or an automatic impulse to sin. They will rather have an impulse to "love God and keep His commandments."

This is because their very *nature* has been transformed so that their desire is only for the things of God.

9. "What shall we say then? Shall we continue in sin that grace may abound? Certainly not! How shall we who died to sin live any longer in it?" (Romans 6:1–2). When have you chosen to sin, telling yourself, "It's okay—God will forgive me"?

....
....
....
....
....
....
....
....
....

10. Paul writes that we have died to sin. How should this apply to your attitude toward temptation? How does being "dead to sin" affect your identity?

....
....
....
....
....
....
....
....
....
....
....

TODAY AND TOMORROW

Today: Jesus redeemed me from slavery to sin,
making me a child of God!

Tomorrow: I will remember that a child of God should
not act like a slave to sin.

CLOSING PRAYER

Father, we thank You and praise You for loving us so much that You chose to send Your Son to the cross to pay the price for our sins. We didn't deserve it. Even when eternity has begun and we are a million years out in serving You, loving You, praising You, and worshipping you, we still will not deserve it! We pray that You will convey this simple childlike truth to us: it's not how we perceive our worth but the value You place on us that determines our worth. And You, Father, say that we are of eternal value. May we believe today who You say that we are in Christ.

Notes and Prayer Requests

Use this space to write any key points, questions, or prayer requests from this week's study.

You Are an Heir with Christ

IN THIS LESSON

Learning: What does it mean to be an heir together with Christ?

Growing: What exactly is my inheritance, and what difference does it make now?

Many people today daydream of receiving an unexpected inheritance from a wealthy person. But the fact is that as a believer in Christ, you *are* the heir of the most lavish inheritance that any person could ever dream to receive. You have a grand inheritance in store for you!

As Paul relates, "In [Christ] also we have obtained an inheritance, being predestined according to the purpose of Him who works all things according to the counsel of His will" (Ephesians 1:11). What is this inheritance? Paul describes it in these terms: "every spiritual blessing in the heavenly places in Christ" (verse 3), "exceeding riches of His grace" (2:7), "treasure in earthen vessels" (2 Corinthians 4:7), and "riches of His glory" (Ephesians 3:16).

Paul also declared, "Eye has not seen, nor ear heard, nor have entered into the heart of man the things which God has prepared for those who love Him" (1 Corinthians 2:9). The inheritance that we have in Christ Jesus is so glorious, so vast, and so tremendous that we cannot comprehend it with our finite minds! God is willing and able "to do exceedingly abundantly above all that we ask or think" (Ephesians 3:20).

The inheritance that God has prepared for us is an overflowing and abundant inheritance. Nothing of benefit or goodness has been withheld from us.

1. What is the most impossible thing that you have ever prayed for? What is the most wonderful miracle that you have ever daydreamed about?

2. God is able to do "exceedingly abundantly above all that we ask or think." What does this say about your inheritance in Christ?

....

....

....

....

....

....

....

....

....

....

....

ARE CHRISTIANS RICH OR POOR?

Many Christians today see themselves as poor. They may have formed this identity because they were taught incorrectly that Christians are supposed to be poor and uneducated. There is no justification for this viewpoint in Scripture. Rather, to the contrary, Paul declares in Philippians 4:19, "My God shall supply all your need according to His riches in glory by Christ Jesus." You are to study the truth of God's Word and be well-informed about your inheritance.

Rich or poor is never a matter of one's bank account. Wealth and poverty are states of the heart. You respond to life with generosity or stinginess, with fear or boldness, with hesitation or with courage, based on how rich you perceive yourself to be in Christ Jesus and how much you trust God to supply your needs. For this reason, your identity must always be based on what you know to be true in God's Word, not on how you feel on any given day or what others say. You must never draw your identity from unbelievers.

Sadly, the reality is that many Christians today look to the world for their identity—and they conclude they are poor or lacking in some way. But the world bases its conclusions on *comparison*. If you compare yourself to others you will always lose, because you will always be able to find somebody who has more or achieves more than you do. God never calls us to compare ourselves to others! He calls us instead to look to Christ Jesus.

God says, "You are in Christ. There is no comparison to those who are in Christ. You have it *all*. Not only now, but forever. Anything of lasting value or great worth, I have given you in Christ Jesus. You have all of Him, and He has all of anything that truly matters!"

3. "The Spirit Himself bears witness with our spirit that we are children of God, and if children, then heirs—heirs of God and joint heirs with Christ, if indeed we suffer with Him, that we may also be glorified together" (Romans 8:16–17). Why do you think that Paul includes suffering as part of our inheritance with Christ?

4. What sufferings were part of Christ's inheritance? How can this knowledge that suffering is part of our inheritance help you understand your true identity?

....

....

....

....

....

....

....

....

....

....

....

You Shall Be Like Christ

The Bible is specific about your inheritance in Christ Jesus. Many things are promised to those who are *in Christ*, but in this lesson, we are going to focus on three things. *First, the Bible promises that you shall be like Christ.* Adults often look at a child and conclude, "He has his father's genes. He is going to look just like his father when he grows up." Or they say, "She has her mother's eyes. She's going to be a beauty just like her mom." We inherit our physical characteristics and attributes from our parents. Similarly, we are destined to mature into the very likeness of Christ Jesus. One day, we are going to be *like Him*.

The disciple John wrote the following to the believers of his day: "Behold what manner of love the Father has bestowed on us, that we should be called children of God! Therefore the world does not know us, because it did not know Him. Beloved, now we are children of God; and it has not yet been revealed what we shall be, but we know that when He is revealed, we shall be like Him, for we shall see Him as He is" (1 John 3:1–2).

Look at this passage and ask yourself, *What did Christ desire that He did not have?* Nothing! *What did Christ want to do that He was incapable of doing?* Nothing! *What did Christ long to possess that He could not possess?* Nothing! To be like Christ is to have all that Christ has, to know all that Christ knows, and to desire all that Christ desires.

5. "For whom He foreknew, He also predestined to be conformed to the image of His Son, that He might be the firstborn among many brethren" (Romans 8:29). What does it mean to be "conformed to the image" of Jesus?

   ....

   ....

   ....

   ....

   ....

   ....

   ....

   ....

   ....

6. What aspects of Christ's character do you see in your own life? How can this influence your sense of identity?

   ....

   ....

   ....

   ....

   ....

   ....

   ....

   ....

   ....

You Will Reign with Christ

Second, not only will you be like Christ, but you will also rule with Christ. Paul stated that God, in His mercy and because of His great love, has "raised us up together" with Christ and "made us sit together in the heavenly places in Christ Jesus" (Ephesians 2:6). Jesus is sitting on His throne in heaven today. In the spiritual realm, as a believer in Christ, you are sitting with Him!

Now, a young prince who is crowned king may not receive the *fullness* of his authority as king until he reaches a certain age. Nevertheless, we still recognize him as the crowned king. The years between the time of his coronation and his assumption of full power are years of growing in preparation and increasing authority. The same is true of your inheritance to "reign with Christ." You are a "joint heir" with Christ, and as you mature in Him, your authority and ability to rule increase. The fullness of your ability to rule begins now . . . but it ends in eternity.

So ask yourself, *Was there any force of evil that was beyond the ability of Jesus to rule over it?* No! *Was any disease greater than the power of Jesus to heal?* No! *Was any demon in a person more powerful than Jesus' power to cast it out?* No! *Was Satan himself more powerful than Jesus?* No! Christ in you makes you more than a conqueror (see Romans 8:37).

7. What experiences in your life might God be using to prepare you to reign with Christ?

8. "Yet in all these things we are more than conquerors through Him who loved us" (Romans 8:37). What does it mean to be "more than conquerors"?

_____

_____

_____

_____

_____

_____

_____

You Will Have a Heavenly Home with Christ

Third, you have the great inheritance of heaven itself. You have been given the character and nature of Christ. You will reign over all things with Him. But you will also receive an eternal home. Jesus said, "I go to prepare a place for you. And if I go and prepare a place for you, I will come again and receive you to Myself; that where I am, there you may be also" (John 14:2–3).

This is your greatest inheritance of all—to be with Christ forever. As John relates, this inherited "family home" is one in which "God will wipe away every tear from [our] eyes; there shall be no more death, nor sorrow, nor crying. There shall be no more pain, for the former things have passed away" (Revelation 21:4). He adds, "There shall be no more curse, but the throne of God and of the Lamb shall be in it, and His servants shall serve Him. . . . There shall be no night there: They need no lamp nor light of the sun, for the Lord God gives them light. And they shall reign forever and ever" (Revelation 22:3, 5).

Peter likewise wrote, "Blessed be the God and Father of our Lord Jesus Christ, who according to His abundant mercy has begotten us again to a living hope through the resurrection of Jesus Christ from the dead, to an inheritance incorruptible and undefiled and that does not fade away, reserved in heaven for you" (1 Peter 1:3–4).

9. How would you define "incorruptible and undefiled" and "does not fade away"?

....
....
....
....
....
....
....
....

10. How do these aspects of your inheritance compare with earthly inheritances?

....
....
....
....
....
....
....
....

THE GUARANTEE OF YOUR FULL INHERITANCE

How can you be assured you *are* an heir? How can you be certain you will receive the full inheritance God has for you? As Paul writes, "You were sealed with the Holy Spirit of promise, who is the guarantee of our inheritance until the redemption of the purchased possession, to the praise of His glory" (Ephesians 1:13–14). The Holy Spirit within you is proof that God has given you a glorious inheritance and that He will bring that inheritance to full fruition.

During biblical times, *seals were used to indicate ownership*. People placed valuable possessions in containers and then attached a seal of ownership to them. You are owned by Christ Jesus—purchased by the price of His shed blood. Seals also *verified an article was genuine*. When the Holy Spirit indwells you, He changes your nature and gives authenticity to the truth that Jesus is your Savior and Lord. Seals *represented authority*. The official scrolls of kings were sealed to indicate the documents were backed by the full authority of the king's power. We are under the authority of God—and no longer under the authority of the devil.

Seals also *represented completed transactions*. Documents were sealed to indicate a transaction had been completed and established in law. The apostle Paul states repeatedly that you *have* obtained an inheritance in Christ. The transaction of your inheritance was fully completed in Christ's death and resurrection. What can break this seal? Nothing. Who can undo what God does? No one. As a believer in Christ, you are sealed forever "according to the good pleasure of His will, to the praise of the glory of His grace" (Ephesians 1:5-6).

It is the work of the Holy Spirit that brings you to the point of *receiving* your full inheritance. There is nothing you can achieve in your own strength. It is only through the *Holy Spirit's* power that you can be brought into the fullness of Christ's character, authority, and wisdom. It is *His* power that resurrects you to eternal life. Your part is simply to trust God, God's Word, listen to the Holy Spirit day by day, and to *obey* what God is calling you to do.

It is in this way that you will become the person that God has designed you to be. The work of the Holy Spirit prepares you to use your inheritance wisely and for the glory of God. He will accomplish this inheritance in His own timing and according to His own methods.

TODAY AND TOMORROW

Today: My inheritance is to be like Christ
and to reign with Him forever.

Tomorrow: I will ask God to teach me how to
be like Jesus more and more.

CLOSING PRAYER

Father, thank You for the promise that You have raised us up and seated us with Christ in the heavenly places. Thank You that You did not abandon us, or leave us helpless and defenseless, but that You took us into Your own family. We are Your adopted children, with all the rights and privileges that come with such an exalted position. We pray our lives will be a testimony to the world of Your grace—so that others may come to be a part of Your family as well.

NOTES AND PRAYER REQUESTS

Use this space to write any key points, questions, or prayer requests from this week's study.

YOU ARE ENLIGHTENED

IN THIS LESSON

Learning: What is my calling?

Growing: How can I find the power that I lack?

Are you aware that you have been given the mind of Christ? It is important for you to recognize this aspect of your identity as a follower of Jesus, for in order to reign with Christ, you need to have both the heart *and* mind of Christ. You must think as He thinks and feel as He feels. You need to possess both His wisdom and His compassion for others.

As Paul writes, the riches of God's grace abound toward us "in all wisdom and prudence" (Ephesians 1:8). God has "made known to us the mystery of His will" and given us "the spirit of wisdom and revelation in the knowledge of Him" (verses 9, 17). Paul's prayer for the Ephesians was for their understanding to be "enlightened; that you may know what is the hope of His calling, what are the riches of the glory of His inheritance in the saints, and what is the exceeding greatness of His power toward us who believe" (verses 18–19).

Ask yourself, *What did Christ want to know that He was incapable of knowing?* Nothing! *What did Christ desire to understand that He could not understand?* Nothing! *What remained a mystery to Christ about God the Father?* Nothing! Just as children grow in their ability to *use* all of the brain cells they are given at birth, so we grow in our ability to understand the deeper things of God *as we grow in our relationship with Christ.* We can have the *mind* of Christ!

1. What passages of Scripture did you once understand differently than you do now? How has your understanding deepened as you have grown in Christ?

2. "Do not be conformed to this world, but be transformed by the renewing of your mind, that you may prove what is that good and acceptable and perfect will of God" (Romans 12:2). How does a person renew his or her mind? How does such a renewal enable us to "prove" God's perfect will?

....

....

....

....

....

....

....

....

....

....

....

....

....

THE HOPE OF GOD'S CALLING

Paul identified three things that we are to know with an *overflowing understanding*: (1) the hope of God's calling, (2) the riches of the glory of Christ's inheritance in the saints, and (3) the exceeding greatness of Christ's power. In this lesson, we are going to look at each of these areas in which we are privileged to experience God's "enlightenment."

First, the hope of God's calling on our lives. Many people say, "I'm not called to be a minister." Most of these people believe that only those who are in full-time ministry are "called." However, the fact is that each of us is called to be a minister—to meet the spiritual, emotional, and physical needs of others. To minister simply means to pray, listen, give wise counsel, share God's Word, love, bless, share our resources, affirm, and basically exercise our ministry gifts given to us by the Holy Spirit. Each of us is called to do this!

In the Bible, we find that believers are given an *upward call*. Paul writes "Brethren, I do not count myself to have apprehended; but one thing I do, forgetting those things which are behind and reaching forward to those things which are ahead, I press toward the goal for the prize of the upward call of God in Christ Jesus" (Philippians 3:13–14). God's call continually compels us to reach for higher moral standards, levels of understanding, character traits, ethical conduct, and degrees of spiritual progress. We are called to grow, develop, and mature in Christ so we might be godly servants. God calls us to be the best that we can be!

The Bible reveals we also have a *holy calling*. Paul wrote to Timothy, "Share with me in the sufferings for the gospel according to the power of God, who has saved us and called us with a holy calling, not according to our works, but according to His own purpose and grace which was given to us in Christ Jesus before time began" (2 Timothy 1:8–9). To be *holy* is to be separated for use by God. It is to be refined so that we no longer think like the world or pursue the lusts of the flesh, the eyes, or the pride of life. It is to view ourselves as agents of righteousness, infusing the world with God's purpose and goodness.

We receive a *heavenly calling*. Our calling is to live a godly life that will influence others to accept Jesus. Everything we do as believers should bear spiritual fruit and have eternal benefit. As the author of Hebrews states, "Holy brethren, partakers of the heavenly calling, consider the Apostle and High Priest of our confession, Christ Jesus" (Hebrews 3:1). We are no longer citizens of this world but citizens of heaven. Our purpose is to pray that God's will be done on earth as it is in heaven. We are to obey the leading of the Holy Spirit so that we will have a part in making God's will a reality on earth.

3. "Therefore, pray: Our Father in heaven, Hallowed be Your name. Your kingdom come. Your will be done on earth as it is in heaven" (Matthew 6:9–10). How is God's will carried out in heaven? How does this compare with the way His will is obeyed on earth?

....
....
....
....
....
....
....
....
....

4. What part do you have in fulfilling this prayer? How does this help define your identity?

....
....
....
....
....
....
....
....

God's Glory in the Inheritance of the Saints

God desires for us to know our *calling* in Christ and to have an understanding about who we are from His perspective. He also desires for us to be enlightened about the "riches of the glory of His inheritance in the saints" (Ephesians 1:18). God gives us all that Christ is, has, and does—His nature, His reign, His eternal life. But what does God give to Christ Jesus as *His* inheritance? Us! The Father says to Jesus, in effect, "Look what a wonderful inheritance I have for You. I have Joe and Roger and Billy for You. I have Sue and Marilyn and Katherine for You."

Many Christians think, "Well, I'm saved, and that's enough." No! You are the inheritance of Christ Jesus. Don't you long to be all that you can be for *His* sake? Don't you desire to present yourself holy before Him—an unblemished and spotless bride? Don't you want to leave behind the "old you" that was in force before you accepted Christ and to become all the "new you" that you can possibly be? When you catch a glimpse of how God regards you, you will place a much higher value on yourself and on all those who are saints with you in Christ Jesus.

5. "Blessed are those who hunger and thirst for righteousness, for they shall be filled" (Matthew 5:6). What does it mean to hunger and thirst for righteousness?

6. How is your appetite for righteousness? What can you do to increase it even more?

....

....

....

....

....

....

....

....

THE GREATNESS OF
GOD'S POWER IN YOU

No believer has justification for saying, "I'm a weakling." As believers in Christ, we have the omnipotent power of God living in us! As Paul writes, we have "the exceeding greatness of His power toward us who believe, according to the working of His mighty power which He worked in Christ when He raised Him from the dead and seated Him at His right hand in the heavenly places, far above all principality and power and might and dominion" (Ephesians 1:19–21).

There is no power greater than the power of the Lord that dwells within us. We have *resurrection power*—the same power that raised Christ from the dead now resides within us. We have *power over spiritual darkness* and *power over the systems of the world,* whether natural, spiritual, or human. "[God] put all things under [Christ's] feet, and gave Him to be head over all things to the church, which is His body" (verses 22–23).

Just as children grow into the full use of their physical strength and ability, so we are growing into our spiritual strength and power in Jesus. Even as we do, we must recognize the Holy Spirit in us is *greater* than any other form of power that we can ever experience.

God in us is greater than anything that can ever come against us (see 1 John 4:4).

So, how do we activate this power of God in our lives? By waiting on Him in quiet trust and by praising Him. Waiting on the Lord brings us to a realization of all He has done for us and all that He is. Praise releases joy into our hearts . . . and the joy of the Lord *is* our strength. We are to know our calling, who we are in Christ, and the power of the Holy Spirit in us—but the greatest "knowing" that we can ever have is "knowing Christ."

This does not mean knowing *about* Christ, but knowing Christ Himself. The more we know Him, the more we know what He wants us to do in every situation. We know our *calling*. The more we know Christ and develop an ever-deepening relationship with Him, the more we value who He is transforming us to be. In that, we know the richness of our own identity. The more we know Christ and rely on Him for daily strength and energy, the more we know His power in us. Knowing Christ is the key—not merely knowing *about* Him.

7. "But you shall receive power when the Holy Spirit has come upon you; and you shall be witnesses to Me in Jerusalem, and in all Judea and Samaria, and to the end of the earth" (Acts 1:8). What power does God's Spirit make available to His children? How can this power in itself be a witness to the world around you?

8. "I am not ashamed, for I know whom I have believed and am persuaded that He is able to keep what I have committed to Him until that Day" (2 Timothy 1:12). How does an intimate knowledge of a person help you to predict what he or she will do? How does an intimate knowledge of Jesus help you trust Him for your future?

....

....

....

....

....

....

....

....

....

....

....

YOUR RESPONSE TO GOD'S ENLIGHTENMENT

So, *why do you need to know that you are called of God?* So that you will have hope about your future and have a direction for your life. *Why do you need to know you are the inheritance of Christ Jesus?* So you will begin to reflect the value that God places on you. *Why do you need to know that you have been given exceedingly great power in the Holy Spirit?* So you will act boldly and be courageous in the face of evil, doubt, and persecution.

The good news is that you are given this wisdom and revelation. God has given you the ability to know, the ability to understand, the ability to discern, and the ability to make sound judgments and wise decisions. The things of God are not a mystery to the believer in Christ! God wants you to have all the information you need to live an effective, successful, and godly life. He does not play a guessing game with His children. He will give you the wisdom that you need, the power that you need, and the esteem that you need.

Your part is to read and study God's Word, come to God in prayer, and seek an abiding relationship with Him. God's part is to bring His Word to life in your spirit and to increase your knowledge and understanding. His part is to guide you into the paths of righteousness. So today, claim this truth about your identity—you are an enlightened saint of God!

9. "For God has not given us a spirit of fear, but of power and of love and of a sound mind" (2 Timothy 1:7). How does the spirit of God bring you power and a sound mind?

....
....
....
....
....
....
....

10. "You are of God, little children, and have overcome them, because He who is in you is greater than he who is in the world" (1 John 4:4). How has having the Holy Spirit residing within you made you different after accepting Christ as your Savior?

....
....
....
....
....
....
....

TODAY AND TOMORROW

Today: I have been called to share in Christ's inheritance and to show forth God's power.

Tomorrow: I will spend time this week in prayer and Bible reading, striving to know Christ better.

CLOSING PRAYER

Father, please work on the inside of us and realign our thinking. You know the areas where we need to receive Your enlightenment—where we need to understand the truths of Your Word. Help us to let go of all pretenses about our own self-worth. Help us to recognize we are just Your children, walking in the Spirit, loving You and being loved by You, moment by moment and day by day. Give us Your mind, we pray, so that we will have Your eyes to see the things in this life that You want us to see. Let us be fountains overflowing with Your truth.

NOTES AND PRAYER REQUESTS

Use this space to write any key points, questions, or prayer requests from this week's study.

YOU ARE PART OF THE BODY

IN THIS LESSON

Learning: Where can I find lasting peace?

Growing: What does it mean to be part of the "body of Christ"?

Do you ever question whether you really fit anywhere? Do you have a firm understanding that you belong as a full member of Christ's body? As Paul writes, the church—which is composed of all true believers in Christ—is "His body, the fullness of Him who fills all in all" (Ephesians 1:23).

Prior to being a part of the body of Christ, you were an individual, alone and isolated. You were not able to enter into a relationship with God, and you were not capable of having a fully reconciled relationship with another human being. Now, it is true that people who aren't in Christ fall in love, get married, make friends, and are in relationships. But this only occurs at a surface level. Without genuine forgiveness and love, no one can truly enter into an abiding relationship with another person. Our abilities to forgive and express love are ultimately drawn from our having received forgiveness and love from God.

Those who are separate from Christ are thus separate from God and from believers. But those who are in Christ are now united together as *one body*. Paul describes this reconciliation when he writes, "Therefore remember that you, once Gentiles in the flesh—who are called Uncircumcision by what is called the Circumcision made in the flesh by hands—that at that time you were without Christ, being aliens from the commonwealth of Israel and strangers from the covenants of promise, having no hope and without God in the world. But now in Christ Jesus you who once were far off have been brought near by the blood of Christ" (2:11-13).

To be "brought near" by the blood of Christ means to enter into an intimate relationship with God and be fully "accepted in the Beloved" (see Ephesians 1:6). To be "brought near" is also a Jewish term relating to the Temple. The courts of the Temple were arranged so the "court of the Gentiles" was farthest from the Holy of Holies, which held the Ark of the Covenant and was the seat of God's presence among the Israelites. The next court was the court of the righteous Jewish women, and the next after that was the court of the righteous Jewish men. The inner court was reserved for those who served as priests before God.

In Christ, believers are brought into the very presence of God—regardless of whether they were originally Jews or Gentiles. Belief in Christ Jesus brings us into the direct presence of God Almighty. Furthermore, Jesus taught that we—as believers in Him—are united completely with Him and with the Father. He prayed the following for us the night He prayed for His disciples: "I do not pray for these alone, but also for those who will believe in Me through their word; that they all may be one, as You, Father, are in Me, and I in You; that they also may be one in Us, that the world may believe that You sent me" (John 17:20–21).

1. How does it make you feel to know that Jesus prayed for you before going to the cross?

....

....

....

....

....

....

....

2. Consider how closely linked Jesus is to God the Father. How does it affect you to realize that you are just as closely linked to the body of Christ?

....

....

....

....

....

....

....

PEACE WITHIN THE BODY

The key word that Paul uses in describing our new identity of belonging to the body of Christ is *peace*. As he writes, "[Jesus] Himself is our peace, who has made both one, and has broken down the middle wall of separation, having abolished in His flesh the enmity, that is, the law of commandments contained in ordinances, so as to create in Himself one new man from the two, thus making peace, and that He might reconcile them both to God in one body through the cross, thereby putting to death the enmity" (Ephesians 2:14–16).

Our ability to be at peace with others flows from Christ, who abides in us as our Peacemaker. No law can ever force two people to be at peace with each other. Again and again, we see worldly peace treaties broken and erupting into wars, because what was drafted on paper had not first been written on the hearts of the people. Again and again, we find individuals claiming they are at peace with each other, only to see that peace shattered by arguments and hostile attitudes. This is because the peace they claimed to have was only on the surface—it was not a true peace that resided in their hearts.

Christ alone makes lasting and genuine peace possible. It is when we recognize and accept His peace within that we can enter into a ministry of reconciliation with others. A ministry of reconciliation means we become peacemakers ourselves—speaking God's peace to those who are sinners and inviting them to enter a reconciled relationship with God. We also speak peace to our fellow believers, so we all might become fully united in the Spirit.

3. What relationships have changed in your own life since becoming a Christian? When have you become reconciled with someone whom you didn't like previously?

4. "Now all things are of God, who has reconciled us to Himself through Jesus Christ, and has given us the ministry of reconciliation, that is, that God was in Christ reconciling the world to Himself, not imputing their trespasses to them, and has committed to us the word of reconciliation" (2 Corinthians 5:18-19). What exactly is "the ministry of reconciliation"? Who has exercised that ministry in your life?

....

....

....

....

....

....

....

....

....

....

....

YOU ARE GOD'S TEMPLE

One of the great illustrations that Paul uses to describe the body of Christ is that of a temple. As he writes, we are all members of the "household of God, having been built on the foundation of the apostles and prophets, Jesus Christ Himself being the chief cornerstone, in whom the whole building, being fitted together, grows into a holy temple in the Lord, in whom you also are being built together for a dwelling place of God in the Spirit" (Ephesians 2:19-22).

The Ephesian believers were living in the shadow of a great temple to the pagan goddess Diana, one of the seven wonders of the ancient world. This temple was built to bring "glory" to the goddess Diana. The Greeks considered the god or goddess who had the greatest temple to be the god or goddess with the greatest importance. After all, the most important god or goddess would surely reside in the most important city on earth. The Ephesians claimed that place of preeminence for themselves because of the temple to Diana.

Paul used this as a springboard for a deeper teaching about the identity of the believer. He said, "You are a holy temple in the Lord." He saw believers as a dwelling place of God in the spirit—a magnificent temple not made with human hands but crafted by Christ Jesus. This temple is eternal. It is magnificent because it is the work of Christ. And it is a temple that is ever growing—more and more believers are simply making it a more and more glorious temple.

This temple of believers is intended for one purpose—to reflect the *glory of God*. It is not intended to draw attention or praise to the believers, either individually or as a group. Rather, it is to focus faith, hope, and love on the One who created it—the Lord Almighty!

5. "Do you not know that you are the temple of God and that the Spirit of God dwells in you?" (1 Corinthians 3:16). What does it mean that "you are the temple of God"? How, in specific terms, should this affect your life?

6. What effect does God's Spirit have on your identity? What effect does it have on your purpose within the body of Christ?

....

....

....

....

....

....

....

....

MANY FUNCTIONS BUT ONE BODY

Even though we are united to other believers in Christ's body, we do not lose our individual identity. Rather, we have the blessed opportunity to express our individual identity and gifts in cooperation with other believers. We are not all the same within the body of Christ . . . but we do have the same purpose. As the apostle Paul wrote:

> For as we have many members in one body, but all the members do not have the same function, so we, being many, are one body in Christ, and individually members of one another. Having then gifts differing according to the grace that is given to us, let us use them: if prophecy, let us prophesy in proportion to our faith; or ministry, let us use it in our ministering; he who teaches, in teaching; he who exhorts, in exhortation; he who gives, with liberality; he who leads, with diligence; he who shows mercy, with cheerfulness (Romans 12:4–8).

We are to give our gifts in acts of ministry. We are to open ourselves up to receiving the ministry gifts of other believers. In this way, we are each made whole *as a body* and grow in our ability to love God and love others.

7. "But, speaking the truth in love, [we] may grow up in all things into Him who is the head—Christ—from whom the whole body, joined and knit together by what every joint supplies, according to the effective working by which every part does its share, causes growth of the body for the edifying of itself in love" (Ephesians 4:15–16). What does Paul mean when he says that "every part does its share" within the body of Christ?

....

....

....

....

....

....

....

....

8. What is the purpose of the body's growth? How is love essential to the body's health?

....

....

....

....

....

....

....

Your Role Within the Body of Christ

The body of Christ simply cannot function if it is scattered and divided. It cannot function unless believers come together and worship the Lord and minister to one another. Again and again, the writers of the New Testament call us to be involved with one another. We are part of a living entity—the body of Christ. We are intended to be in close relationship and to function together as a whole. Just read what the writers of the Bible have said:

> I plead with you, brethren, by the name of our Lord Jesus Christ, that you all speak the same thing, and that there be no divisions among you, but that you be perfectly joined together in the same mind and in the same judgment (1 Corinthians 1:10).

> Do not be drunk with wine, in which is dissipation; but be filled with the Spirit, speaking to one another in psalms and hymns and spiritual songs, singing and making melody in your heart to the Lord, giving thanks always for all things to God the Father in the name of our Lord Jesus Christ, submitting to one another in the fear of God (Ephesians 5:18–21).

> Therefore comfort each other and edify one another, just as you also are doing. And we urge you, brethren, to recognize those who labor among you, and are over you in the Lord and admonish you, and to esteem them very highly in love for their work's sake. Be at peace among yourselves (1 Thessalonians 5:11–13).

> And let us consider one another in order to stir up love and good works, not forsaking the assembling of ourselves together, as is the manner of some, but exhorting one another, and so much the more as you see the Day approaching (Hebrews 10:24–25).

> Is anyone among you sick? Let him call for the elders of the church, and let them pray over him, anointing him with oil

in the name of the Lord. And the prayer of faith will save the sick, and the Lord will raise him up. And if he has committed sins, he will be forgiven. Confess your trespasses to one another, and pray for one another, that you may be healed. The effective, fervent prayer of a righteous man avails much (James 5:14–16).

Our function as members of Christ's body is thus threefold: (1) to build up the body of Christ, (2) to create a sense of belonging for all believers, and (3) to bring glory to the Lord. If we have an identity as part of the body of Christ, we will do everything possible to function as part of that body. And in functioning as members in His body, we grow in our own sense of belonging and enjoy reconciliation and fellowship with others.

9. "For as we have many members in one body, but all the members do not have the same function, so we, being many, are one body in Christ, and individually members of one another" (Romans 12:4–5). What does it mean that Christians are "members of one another"? Give examples of how you have seen this in practice.

10. "And let us consider one another in order to stir up love and good works" (Hebrews 10:24). Why is it so important for Christians to consider "one another" in every way?

....

....

....

....

....

....

TODAY AND TOMORROW

Today: Being a part of the body of Christ means that I must do my part and work to live at peace with others.

Tomorrow: I will ask the Lord to teach me more fully what my role is as a member of the body of Christ.

CLOSING PRAYER

Father, we thank You for the brothers and sisters in Christ that You have placed in our lives. Give us today an increased sense of oneness and fellowship with them. We want to sense each other's needs and be a living example of what the church was designed to be—the Temple of the Holy Spirit and the body of Christ. We pray our lives will be so lived together in oneness—in unity and fellowship— that the helpless, the hopeless, and the alienated will be drawn to You.

NOTES AND PRAYER REQUESTS

Use this space to write any key points, questions, or prayer requests from this week's study.

You Are a Vessel for Ministry

IN THIS LESSON

Learning: What is my purpose in life?

Growing: How can I learn to do good works?

As believers in Christ, we are members of a living body. In a practical way, we are the "hands and feet" of the Lord on the earth today. Christ works through our hands to touch a sick person, clothe someone in need, and hand a cup of cold water to a thirsty person. Christ walks with our feet into areas of need. Christ speaks through our mouths His words of comfort and edification.

We have a great and glorious purpose on earth. We are to be agents of God's love, ambassadors for Christ, and the initiators of good works. We are to pour out our lives in service to others, just as Christ gave Himself for us. As Paul writes, "Be imitators of God as dear children. And walk in love, as Christ also has loved us and given Himself for us, an offering and a sacrifice to God for a sweet-smelling aroma" (Ephesians 5:1–2).

Works can never save us, can never purchase our forgiveness, and can never qualify us to receive God's love. Yet good works are the natural outcome of our salvation. Once we have been born again, our natural impulse is toward good works. Paul also wrote, "For you were once darkness, but now you are light in the Lord. Walk as children of light (for the fruit of the Spirit is in all goodness, righteousness, and truth), finding out what is acceptable to the Lord" (Ephesians 5:8–10).

Jesus walked this earth healing the sick and brokenhearted, preaching good tidings to the poor, proclaiming liberty to the captives, giving hope to the oppressed, and comforting those who mourn. He even announced this as His mission: "The Spirit of the Lord is upon Me, because He has anointed Me to preach the gospel to the poor; He has sent Me to heal the brokenhearted, to proclaim liberty to the captives and recovery of sight to the blind, to set at liberty those who are oppressed; to proclaim the acceptable year of the Lord" (Luke 4:18–19).

We are to follow in Jesus' footsteps and do the same. He calls today and commissions us to His ministry, just as He commissioned the disciples: "And He called the twelve to Himself, and began to send them out two by two, and gave them power over unclean spirits. . . . So they went out and preached that people should repent. And they cast out many demons, and anointed with oil many who were sick, and healed them" (Mark 6:7, 12–13).

1. "When He had called His twelve disciples to Him, He gave them power over unclean spirits, to cast them out, and to heal all kinds of sickness and all kinds of disease" (Matthew 10:1).

What power did the disciples have that enabled them to cast out demons and heal the sick?

....

....

....

....

....

....

....

....

2. Think of two or three people whom you know who are sick or discouraged. How can you minister to them this week?

....

....

....

....

....

....

....

....

YOU ARE CREATED FOR GOOD WORKS

Paul writes that we are God's workmanship, "created in Christ Jesus for good works, which God prepared beforehand that we should walk in them" (Ephesians 2:10). God made us with a purpose in mind. He had a plan for our lives from before the foundation of the world—a plan that we are uniquely designed to fulfill. "He chose us in Him before the foundation of the world, that we should be holy and without blame before Him in love" (1:4).

The Lord knows precisely the good works that we are capable of doing, and also those which we will excel in doing, which will give us a great sense of satisfaction. A *good work* is any work that reflects Jesus and brings glory to God. *Good* is the same word that God used in evaluating each aspect of creation: "And God saw that it was good" (Genesis 1:10, 12, 18, 25). The creative work of God is not finished. It is ongoing by the power of the Holy Spirit in our lives. God continues to shine light into darkness, to bring forth good out of evil, and order out of confusion, and purpose out of things that seem meaningless.

One of the best-known verses in all the Bible declares, "All things work together for good to those who love God, to those who are the called according to His purpose" (Romans 8:28). No matter what happens to us or around us, the Holy Spirit is capable of producing a *good work* in us and through us. We were created for good works!

3. "Be doers of the word, and not hearers only, deceiving yourselves. For if anyone is a hearer of the word and not a doer, he is like a man observing his natural face in a mirror; for he observes himself, goes away, and immediately forgets what kind of man he was" (James 1:22–24). What does it mean to be a "doer of the word?" When have you known you were doing what God had created you to do? What were the results?

4. How do believers in Christ deceive themselves if they are "hearers only" of God's word?

....

....

....

....

....

....

....

....

....

....

....

....

YOU CAN RECEIVE GOD'S STRENGTH

Many Christians say about themselves, "I'm not capable of ministry." The fact is, none of us are capable by ourselves. But with Christ, all things are possible. As Paul writes, "God has not given us a spirit of fear, but of power and of love and of a sound mind" (2 Timothy 1:7), and "[We] can do all things through Christ who strengthens [us]" (Philippians 4:13).

God supplies what we are lacking. When we are weak, He gives us the strength to be strong. When we are without resources, He supplies what is needed to accomplish what He has set out for us to do. When we are without courage, He gives us the ability to endure and to be bold. Again and again in the Bible, we have examples of those who *could not* accomplish the work in their own ability, but who *could* as they received the strength of the Lord.

Paul wrote about a painful "thorn in the flesh" that He asked the Lord repeatedly to take away from his life. As he wrote to the Corinthians, "Concerning this thing I pleaded with the Lord three times that it might depart from me. And He said to me, 'My grace is sufficient for you, for My strength is made perfect in weakness.' Therefore most gladly I will rather boast in my infirmities, that the power of Christ may rest upon me. Therefore I take pleasure in infirmities, in reproaches, in needs, in persecutions, in distresses, for Christ's sake. For when I am weak, then I am strong" (2 Corinthians 12:8–10).

5. "God is able to make all grace abound toward you, that you, always having all sufficiency in all things, may have an abundance for every good work" (2 Corinthians 9:8). Why do we need an abundance of grace for every good work?

6. What does God's grace have to do with our good works? How does the calling to good works influence your identity?

....

....

....

....

....

....

....

....

....

....

....

YOUR IDENTITY
AS GOD'S WITNESS

We are created for good works, and we are also called to be Christ's witnesses. We are to proclaim the good news of His death and resurrection— and to be bold in telling others about God's love, mercy, grace, and free offer of forgiveness and eternal life. We have been given a "good message" to proclaim to accompany our "good works"!

In the book of Acts, we read how the disciples Peter and John were put into prison for proclaiming that Jesus was the Messiah. They were called before the religious leaders in Jerusalem the next day and told to stop proclaiming the message of the gospel. But Peter and John answered, "We cannot but speak the things which we have seen and heard" (Acts 4:20). They were released with further threats, and they returned to their fellow believers.

After Peter and John had related all that had happened, the disciples prayed this: "Now, Lord, look on their threats, and grant to Your servants that with all boldness they may speak Your word" (verse 29). What was the result? "They spoke the word of God with boldness" and the "multitude of those who believed were of one heart and one soul" (verses 31–32).

7. "Go therefore and make disciples of all the nations, baptizing them in the name of the Father and of the Son and of the Holy Spirit, teaching them to observe all things that I have commanded you; and lo, I am with you always, even to the end of the age" (Matthew 28:19–20). Jesus commands His followers to teach others "to observe all things that I have commanded." What is required if you are to teach that to others?

....

....

....

....

....

....

....

....

....

....

8. How does this responsibility affect your self-identity?

....

....

....

....

....

....

....

....

....

....

Your Identity as God's Ambassador

We are God's ambassadors when we are doing good works and proclaiming the "good news" of Christ. As Paul writes in 2 Corinthians 5:20, "We are ambassadors for Christ, as though God were pleading through us." We are citizens of heaven, sojourning on this earth in temporary "tents"—our physical bodies. We are "fellow citizens with the saints" who have gone before us (see Ephesians 2:19). Our true home is in heaven.

When we see ourselves as citizens of an everlasting kingdom—residing only temporarily on this earth to speak the good news of Christ and do good works—we will have a new perspective on our possessions, our commitments and agendas, and our use of time and resources. Our priorities will change. No longer will we see ourselves as needing to accomplish human-made goals, or cling to material things, or feel the need to achieve fame and power in this world. When we have a firm identity that we are citizens of heaven, ambassadors for Christ on earth, we will make the most of our earthly time and resources for eternal reward!

Do you truly see yourself as a vessel of God intended for His purposes of ministry on this earth—purposes that involve doing good works and proclaiming the good news? If not, ask the Lord to help you see yourself as He sees you. He does not intend for you to just "slide" through life until you land on the other side in eternity. No! You have work to do and a message to proclaim . . . and today is the day to start doing what God has called you to do.

9. "Do not lay up for yourselves treasures on earth, where moth and rust destroy and where thieves break in and steal; but lay up for yourselves treasures in heaven, where neither moth nor rust destroys and where thieves do not break in and steal. For where your treasure is, there your heart will be also" (Matthew 6:19–21).

What do you treasure most in life? What does it mean to "lay up treasures in heaven"?

....

....

....

....

....

....

....

10. "Every good tree bears good fruit, but a bad tree bears bad fruit. A good tree cannot bear bad fruit, nor can a bad tree bear good fruit" (Matthew 7:17–18). What sort of fruit is your life bearing? What will you do this week to bear more "good fruit"?

....

....

....

....

....

....

....

TODAY AND TOMORROW

Today: I am called to be both a witness and an ambassador for Christ to the world around me.

Tomorrow: I will cultivate good fruit in my life and cut out the bad fruit.

CLOSING PRAYER

. . . .

Father, we pray that we would not attempt to be conformed to this world—to be shaped into its mold—but simply that we would attempt to walk by faith. We thank You for the example of Jesus, who came into this world not to be served but to serve. Let us follow in His steps today and choose to love and minister to those whom You place in our path. Use us today as Your hands and feet to share the blessed message of the gospel. We ask this in Your name.

NOTES AND
PRAYER REQUESTS

Use this space to write any key points, questions, or prayer requests from this week's study.

YOU ARE CALLED FOR HOLINESS

IN THIS LESSON

Learning: What does it mean for me to live as someone who is "holy"?

Growing: How do I walk in a way that represents my new status as a holy vessel rather than my old life?

As we begin this lesson, I want you to imagine that you are walking on the beach. Imagine striding down the shoreline with the ocean on your left and the dry sand to your right. You are walking right next to the surf, and when the waves come rolling in, the water splashes over your bare feet. That is how close you are to the surf. Can you picture it? Can you hear the crash of the waves and feel the salt breeze against your skin?

Now imagine turning around and looking behind you. What do you see stretching out behind you on that beach? *Footprints.* When you walk on sand, the weight of your body presses down against the ground and leaves an imprint. If you wanted, you could reverse course and trace your steps back to where you started, because you've impacted the ground in that way.

Keep this idea in your mind as you read these words from the apostle Paul: "I, therefore, the prisoner of the Lord, beseech you to walk worthy of the calling with which you were called" (Ephesians 4:1). This idea of walking *worthy* means doing it in a way that carries weight. It means walking in such a way that you make an impact on the world, leaving footprints behind just as you would do if you were striding down a sandy beach.

In the previous lesson, we saw that your identity in Christ means that you are a *holy* vessel sanctified by your Master. You are useful to Christ and have been prepared for good works by Him. You are not common, profane, or simplistic in any way, but holy just as God is holy. But how does this impact your everyday life? Specifically, what does it look like for you to walk in a way that is *holy*? What does it mean for you to lead a holy life?

As we will see in this lesson, the answer has a lot to do with that image of footprints on the beach. Walking in holiness means to walk in a way that is *weighty*. It means to live in a way that makes an impact in the world that all who know you can see and experience.

1. How would you describe what it means to lead a holy life?

2. Who are some people that come to mind as examples of holy living? What makes their particular example stand out to you?

....

....

....

....

....

....

....

....

....

....

PUT AWAY YOUR OLD LIFE

The apostle Paul urged believers to "keep the unity of the Spirit in the bond of peace" (Ephesians 4:3). He stated that God has given each of us certain gifts "for the equipping of the saints for the work of ministry, for the edifying of the body of Christ" (verse 12). He showed how we have been "joined and knit together" (verse 16) so we can build up one another.

Paul then states, "This I say, therefore, and testify in the Lord, that you should no longer walk as the rest of the Gentiles walk" (verse 17). The word *therefore* is always important when we encounter it in Scripture. In this case, Paul was referencing everything he had just taught about unity in the church and the use of spiritual gifts for our mutual benefit. He then said, *therefore*, look at your walk . . . *therefore,* look at the way you live.

Here is how Paul put it: "No longer walk as the rest of the Gentiles walk, in the futility of their mind, having their understanding darkened, being alienated from the life of God, because of the ignorance that is in them, because of the blindness of their heart" (verses

17-18). Remember that Paul was writing to Christians in the city of Ephesus—a place filled with enticements, idolatry, and many other opportunities for sin. The believers there were mainly Gentiles, which means they had not grown up with the law and the boundaries of Judaism.

Paul knew his audience would be under pressure from the surrounding community and from the larger society of the Roman Empire with all its carnality and polytheism. So, he said, essentially, "Pay attention to how you walk." Meaning, pay attention to your way of life. Don't allow yourself to be dragged back toward the mess from which you came.

Specifically, Paul wanted the Christians in Ephesus to put away their old way of life. That life had been defined by a *futility* of mind, an understanding that was *darkened, ignorance,* and spiritual *blindness.* He reminded them that those whose lives were void of any meaningful connection to God had no real sense of purpose. They are blinded to the truth.

The reality is that people can have money, power, influence, and seem like a success on every level to those around them. However, if they have no understanding of God's spiritual truth, everything else they possess will be of little value. It is temporary and will not last. We all used to be that way. We were blind, ignorant, and futile in our thinking. But we were called to something immeasurably greater when we heard the gospel and made our choice to follow Christ. Therefore, Paul states, we need to put away our old way of life.

We live in a society that is blind, ignorant, and moving deeper into chaos every day. We live in a culture that promotes getting more and more money and making ourselves more comfortable—keeping ourselves more entertained and appeased. There is a darkness over our world . . . and most of us grew up as part of that darkness. We received the light of Christ when we were saved, but there is still a danger of drifting back toward what was old. So, a major element of walking in holiness is rejecting our old way of life.

3. What are some actions or attitudes that defined your old way of life before Christ?

....

....

....

....

....

....

....

....

4. When do you feel most tempted or pulled to return to those actions and attitudes?

....

....

....

....

....

....

....

....

EMBRACE THE NEW LIFE

Paul continues by setting up a dramatic contrast between the way we used to walk and the way we are now to walk as followers of Christ. As he relates, "put off, concerning your former conduct, the old man which grows corrupt according to the deceitful lusts, and be renewed in the spirit of your mind, and that you put on the new man which was created according to God, in true righteousness and holiness" (Ephesians 4:22–24).

Paul tells us to "put off" our old way of life. Put it aside. Remove it. Let go of it. Get rid of it completely. In its place, we are to "put on the new man," which are the ways of Christ. We are to put on "true righteousness and holiness." We can do this because we have experienced the transformation that comes as a result of the Holy Spirit residing in our lives. "The Helper, the Holy Spirit, whom the Father will send in My name, He will teach you all things, and bring to your remembrance all things that I said to you" (John 14:26).

Perhaps you have wondered whether you really can be changed . . . if you really can get clean before the Lord. If sin has been a major part of your life for much of your life, it can lead you to doubt whether you have the capacity to live the kind of holy life that God requires. But the reality is you *don't* have the capacity, but God certainly does and can empower you to lead that kind of existence in Him. You *absolutely* can walk in holiness. As Paul concludes, the "new man" you are to put on "was created according to God" (Ephesians 4:24). It is God who equips you to walk in holiness and who enables you to embrace this way of life.

5. What are some words that best describe your life after choosing to follow Christ?

6. In what ways do you access God's power to live a "new life" defined by holiness?

....

....

....

....

....

....

....

....

....

....

....

SEPARATE YOURSELF FROM SIN

Sin is a foreign element in the life of every follower of Christ. Once we receive salvation, it is no longer a natural part of our identity. There is no connection point between sin and righteousness . . . they don't fit together. In the same way, we no longer "fit" with sin.

Paul writes, "What fellowship has righteousness with lawlessness? And what communion has light with darkness" (2 Corinthians 6:14). None. Where is the connection between good and evil? There is none. What fellowship exists between Christ and Satan? None. Rather, we have "become the righteousness of God in [Christ]" (5:21). God Himself is living in us, indwelling us through the Holy Spirit. Holiness and righteousness have become a part of who we are. They serve as the foundation of our identity through the power of God.

Now, this does not mean we will never sin again once we receive Christ as our Savior. Obviously, we all know this is not true. We will all struggle with the presence of sin this side of the grave. We will all make mistakes from time to time. But sin should never be *tolerated*. We have become Christ-centered rather than self-centered.

When you do sin, you need to deal with it immediately. Confess and repent of your mistakes. Don't allow Satan to develop a foothold or stronghold. Don't allow anything to fester. Do not have anything to do with it. As Paul said, "You have not so learned Christ" (Ephesians 4:20).

There was a time when you were hardened to sin, but now, by the grace of God, you are sensitive to its presence. You cannot allow the old life—the old self—to once again overwhelm you so you find yourself doing the same old things, thinking the same old thoughts, and acting the same old ways. No! You are a different person.

So throw off the old self and put on the new. You have been made holy in Christ. Your holiness means you are now separated from sin.

7. Do you agree that sin is a foreign element in your life? Explain.

8. Where are you most in danger of being dragged back into old patterns of sin?

RENEW YOUR MIND

Paul didn't just write about holiness to the church in Ephesus. He gave similar instructions in most of his epistles, including his epistle to the Romans. Here is what he writes on the subject to that group of believers: "Brethren, by the mercies of God . . . present your bodies a living sacrifice, holy, acceptable to God, which is your reasonable service. And do not be conformed to this world, but be transformed by the renewing of your mind, that you may prove what is that good and acceptable and perfect will of God" (Romans 12:1–2).

Walking in holiness means offering your entire life as a *holy* and *acceptable* sacrifice to God. It means living each day as an act of worship to God. How do you accomplish this? In Paul's words, "By the renewing of your mind." You must refresh your thinking so you see the world the way God sees it and react in the ways He wants you to react. You become "transformed" in your relationship to the world and "prove" the will of God for your life.

Most of us do not live in a region that is outwardly evil and idolatrous the way it was for ancient Ephesus and Rome. There is a veneer of civilization and respectability in our culture. Still, the modern world is plenty evil and idolatrous. Everywhere we look, it seems as if we are being pushed, pulled, and squeezed by society in an effort to make us conform to this world.

Living in holiness means resisting those efforts. Look again at Paul's words to the Ephesian believers. He describes those "who, being past feeling, have given themselves over to lewdness, to work all uncleanness with greediness" (4:19). The phrase "given themselves over" is important in this verse. In this life, we are going to give ourselves over to something. Either we will give in to the pressures of this world and the desires of sin, or we will give ourselves over to the righteousness and holiness that have taken up residence through Christ. It must be one or the other. We can't have a little sin mixed in with a little righteousness.

Living in holiness means making a conscious decision to give ourselves over to God. Moreover, this is a decision we need to make every day. Every day, we can choose to walk in holiness by offering ourselves to God as a living sacrifice. All our decisions. All our actions. All our thoughts. Even all our emotions. When we give these things completely over to God, He will renew our minds. He will equip us and empower us to walk in holiness.

9. What are some ways that you have experienced the renewing of your mind?

10. How will you set up a time and place to "give yourself" over to holiness each day?

TODAY AND TOMORROW

Today: I will choose to walk in holiness because I have been made holy through Christ.

Tomorrow: I will intentionally and willfully give myself to God each day for the renewing of my mind.

CLOSING PRAYER

Father, we bless You and praise You for calling us to walk in Your holiness. We know that the gift of righteousness is ours to obtain through Christ. Today, we choose to allow Jesus in all of His holiness to rule, to reign, to direct, to dominate, and to guide our lives. May we seek to always walk in righteousness. May our lives reflect the holy life of Christ. Guide us to not excuse sin or rationalize it away, but to face it for what it is, deal with it, and then walk in Your light.

NOTES AND PRAYER REQUESTS

Use this space to write any key points, questions, or prayer requests from this week's study.

YOU ARE A RECIPIENT OF GOD'S RICHES

Learning: What riches can I receive
as a disciple of Jesus?

Growing: What steps can I take to take
hold of everything God has set aside for me
because of my identity in Christ?

Did you ever search for buried treasure as a child? I think about all of us have hoped to stumble onto some buried treasure at some point. Maybe we thought about finding an old pirate's map like Jim Hawkins in *Treasure Island*—"X marks the spot." Maybe we dreamed about tracking down the end of a rainbow to find that fabled pot of gold.

Maybe we rubbed a bunch of lamps or lanterns for a season, hoping a genie would pop out and give us our three wishes.

The specifics don't matter. It's the idea of buried treasure that is so compelling . . . untold riches just sitting out there, waiting to be discovered. After all, who wouldn't want to be going about their ordinary lives and then—*bang*! Gold and silver and diamonds and jewelry and doubloons and all the rest. It's a wonderful dream.

Unfortunately, I cannot tell you how to find buried treasure in the typical sense. But the truth is that you already have access to something much more wonderful and much more incredible than physical treasure. As a child of God, you are a recipient of His riches!

Paul wrote about these riches in his prayer for the Ephesians: "I bow my knees to the Father of our Lord Jesus Christ . . . that He would grant you, according to the riches of His glory, to be strengthened with might through His Spirit in the inner man, that Christ may dwell in your hearts through faith; that you, being rooted and grounded in love, may be able to comprehend with all the saints what is the width and length and depth and height—to know the love of Christ which passes knowledge; that you may be filled with all the fullness of God" (3:14–19).

Now, that is a prayer! God has blessed you according to the riches of His glory. Most people think of material wealth when they think of "riches," but the riches that God offers are so much greater. They cannot be measured by a calculator, purchased with money, or sold on the market. Furthermore, they are available to every person, as Paul had explained: "Blessed be the God and Father of our Lord Jesus Christ, who has blessed us with every spiritual blessing in the heavenly places in Christ, just as He chose us in Him before the foundation of the world, that we should be holy and without blame before Him in love" (Ephesians 1:3–4).

If you are a follower of Christ, then you have already received God's riches. He set them aside for you "before the foundation of the world." You are incredibly rich!

1. What are some of the benefits you have received as a child of God?

....
....
....
....
....
....
....
....
....
....
....
....

2. "My God shall supply all your need according to His riches in glory by Christ Jesus" (Philippians 4:19). What are some needs that you need God to supply from His riches?

....
....
....
....
....
....
....
....
....
....
....
....
....
....
....

YOUR RICHES
MUST BE CLAIMED

Note that Paul described these riches of Christ in a prayer that he offered on behalf of the believers in Ephesus. He said, "For this reason I bow my knees to the Father of our Lord Jesus Christ" (3:14). Now, that might make you question his statements. These words came from a specific individual (Paul) and were prayed on behalf of another specific group of individuals (the church in Ephesus). So, do they really have anything to do with us at all?

In fact, Paul's prayer is an expression of the mind of God. Remember, Paul wrote all of his letters under the inspiration of the Holy Spirit. This means the Holy Spirit was—and is—the source of his prayers. Paul was expressing what the Holy Spirit wanted to accomplish for the believers in Ephesus, which is the same as He wants to accomplish for *all* Christians, including you and me. He desires for us to receive the riches set aside for us.

Paul expounds on this idea of *riches* in his letter of Ephesians. He writes that in Christ "we have redemption through His blood, the forgiveness of sins, according to the riches of His grace" (1:7). He expresses his hope that "in the ages to come [God] might show the exceeding riches of His grace in His kindness toward us in Christ Jesus" (2:7). He states his mission as an apostle is to "preach among the Gentiles the unsearchable riches of Christ" (3:8).

Paul grounded his prayer for the Ephesians on the truth that these riches have their source in God. Everything Paul is about to say is built on the foundation of who God is . . . not who we are. He is describing the unfathomable riches of the omnipotent God, and he expresses his hope that we will claim those riches as our own.

Again, you have *already been given access* to God's riches. They were yours the moment you accepted salvation. You have access to the most incredible buried treasure imaginable . . . and you don't even have to dig it up! Everything has already been provided for you. But you must claim those riches as your own. You must take hold of them and make them yours.

3. In what sense does your relationship with God provide you access to "riches"?

....

....

....

....

....

....

....

....

....

....

4. Are you taking full advantage of your connection to and relationship with the infinite and omnipotent God? Explain.

....

....

....

....

....

....

....

....

....

....

YOUR RICHES ARE INTERNAL

Paul asked that "[God] would grant you, according to the riches of His glory, to be strengthened with might through His Spirit in the inner man" (Ephesians 3:16). Paul asked for you to be "strengthened with might." In the original Greek, those words mean "to become mighty." That's an incredible gift! When you are willing to take hold of what is yours, the Holy Spirit will work in such a way that you become mighty. You will be filled with God's own strength.

Furthermore, Paul also said you can "know the love of Christ which passes knowledge; that you may be filled with all the fullness of God" (verse 19). You can know that which is unknowable . . . namely, the love of Christ. You can feel the love that Christ has for you. It is the same love that led Him to die on the cross as a sacrifice for your sins. You can experience that love when you claim your rightful inheritance as a child of God. And when you experience that love, you will be filled "with all the fullness of God." Those are riches beyond belief!

Notice that what Paul was describing in his prayer applies to "the inner man" (verse 16). In other words, God's riches are internal rather than external. They connect with your spirit. The truth is that many Christians today focus on their *external* reality, including their physical bodies. We all like to decorate ourselves, and get cleaned up, and look a certain way. I'm not saying there's no value in eating right and exercising and being healthy. Our bodies are the "temple of the Holy Spirit" (1 Corinthians 6:19), and we have a responsibility to care for them.

But we need to remember our bodies are *temporary*. The reality is that you should focus most of your attention on what is inside of you—on your spirit rather than your body—because your spirit is eternal. The way you invest in the inner man is to read God's Word, pray, meditate on the Scriptures, memorize them, and practice the spiritual disciplines.

Always remember the real you is deep down inside. It's the "inner man," the inner person, not what's external. That is where the Holy Spirit really works.

5. What are some ways you have developed or invested in your inner self this week?

....

....

....

....

....

....

....

....

....

....

6. What are some ways you have invested in your external, physical body this week?

....

....

....

....

....

....

....

....

Your Riches Include Christ's Presence Within You

Paul described another aspect of God's riches when he said "that Christ may dwell in your hearts through faith" (Ephesians 3:17). One of the reasons you need to focus on the inner man—on your heart—is because Christ dwells inside you. Christ makes His home in your heart.

Have you ever spent time at someone's home and felt a little uncomfortable there? Maybe it was a weekend, or even just a single night, but you wondered, *"Did I come at a bad time? Do they even want me to be here right now? I don't feel welcome here."* Here's an important question: *does Jesus feel comfortable in your life?*

When you become aware that Jesus is dwelling within you—that the very life of God is present inside you—you will change how you live. You will change not only what you do but also the ways you think. The more you are aware of Christ's presence, the more you will understand that stooping down to the level of sin is beneath you. Sin does not match who you are in Christ. Sin does not reflect the One who is living within you.

The Greek word that Paul used for *dwell* referred to a permanent residence. Christ's dwelling in your heart is a permanent situation. He has set up His home in you and His home in your heart. What a blessing! What an expression of God's riches! Yet also a reminder for us to live in a way that we reflect His presence rather than making Him uncomfortable in our hearts.

7. In general terms, do you think Christ is comfortable or uncomfortable with your life? Explain.

8. What are some ways your actions and attitudes would change if you were fully aware of God's presence inside you?

....

....

....

....

....

....

....

YOUR RICHES ARE ROOTED AND GROUNDED IN LOVE

Finally, in talking about the riches you can access because of your identify in Christ, the apostle Paul prayed "that you, being rooted and grounded in love, may be able to comprehend with all the saints what is the width and length and depth and height" of God's love (Ephesians 3: 17–18).

I love that phrase "rooted and grounded." The term *rooted* for me speaks of growth and fruit. God's love is incredibly fruitful. The term *grounded* speaks of strength and stability. You have a firm foundation when you know God's love. Your entire life—your thoughts, words, and deeds—are motivated by love when you are firmly rooted and grounded in Christ's love. You are governed by love, guided by love, and guarded by love.

Let me tell you . . . if you do not know how to love, there will be a host of God's truths that you will never be able to grasp. There will be aspects of God's life that you will never experience. This is because "God is love" (1 John 4:16). You will never understand the depth of everything that God desires for you until you learn how to love.

I am not talking here about a worldly view of love. I'm not talking about affection. I'm talking about the love Jesus highlighted when He said, "By this all will know that you are My disciples, if you have love for one another" (John 13:35). I am talking about the love of God flowing through your life in a way that changes things—that changes others and changes you. This is what happens when you are rooted and grounded in God's love.

Many people today have an intellectual understanding of love. They can describe it, talk about it, and even comprehend it on the level of facts and definitions. But what Paul was talking about is comprehending God's love on a spiritual level. He is talking about experiencing God's love in everyday life . . . not merely understanding the definition of the word.

Can you think of anything better than a life defined by God's love? Can you think of a better mission than being motivated by love in all your actions? This is what I want for my life: *to be rooted and grounded in God's love.* I want my emotions to be governed by love. I want my character to be founded in love. I want my conversations and my conduct not simply to be sprinkled with love but actually salted by love—to be permeated and saturated by it.

You can experience that kind of life, because just like those Christians in Ephesus, you are a child of God. This is your identity in Christ. You can have the love of God flowing through you like a fountain, abounding and gushing forth to cover everyone around you. The only question is . . . *will you take advantage of that opportunity and grab hold of that treasure?*

9. Who comes to mind when you think of someone rooted and grounded in God's love?

10. What obstacles are currently preventing you from experiencing and showing God's love to a greater degree?

....

....

....

....

....

....

....

TODAY AND TOMORROW

Today: I will claim the riches I have been given.

Tomorrow: I will help others understand and experience the depth and breadth and height of God's love.

CLOSING PRAYER

Father, thank You for making us so rich in Christ. We know the great cost this involved—You coming to earth in the form of humanity, stretching out Your loving arms on an old Roman cross, and having those spikes cut through the tendons and the muscle and the fiber. Your precious blood was spilled for our sake. But with every drop came our salvation, our redemption, our forgiveness—all was wrapped up in the shedding of that blood. We cannot comprehend the incredible riches we have obtained in Christ. We simply praise Your holy name that we are so rich because of our relationship to You.

NOTES AND
PRAYER REQUESTS

. . . .

Use this space to write any key points, questions, or prayer requests from this week's study.

YOU ARE GOD'S MASTERPIECE

IN THIS LESSON

Learning: What does it mean to be complete in Christ?

Growing: How can I go from being a mess to a masterpiece?

Are you aware that you are God's masterpiece? As Paul states, "We are His workmanship, created in Christ Jesus for good works" (Ephesians 2:10). The Greek word translated as *workmanship* is *poiema*, from which we get our English words *poem* and *poetry*. It means "something made" and might also be translated as *masterpiece*. We are God's supreme "work in progress"—a work that will culminate in perfection.

A masterpiece is a work of notable excellence. From the very first chapter in the Bible, we see that God considered humankind to be the crowning achievement of His creation. Of all God's creatures, only humans were fashioned in God's own image: "God said, 'Let us make man in our image, according to Our likeness'" (Genesis 1:26). Only humans were made capable of spiritual growth and development, reasoning, faith, learning concepts and principles, making sound decisions and wise judgments, planning for a future, and remembering the details of the past. God breathed into humans His own breath, His essence, His presence. God gave humans a will with which to discern good from evil and to choose between the two options.

It makes a difference whether you see yourself as a mess or a masterpiece. If you believe that you are worthless—without potential and without any hope of excellence—you are likely to give up, become dejected, and become "sick of life." On the other hand, if you believe you are a masterpiece in the making—with vast potential for excellence—you are going to have hope, enthusiasm for life, and a desire to pursue all that God has for you!

REFLECT GOD'S PERFECTION

As we have stated repeatedly in this study, we are believers *in Christ*. Christ Himself is our identity. Here is what Paul said about Christ: "He is the image of the invisible God" (Colossians 1:15). Jesus Christ was the appearance of God in human form so that we might see the perfection of God in a human likeness to which we could relate fully.

So, if we are *in Christ*, we are to reflect God's perfection in human form. Paul writes, "It pleased the Father that in Him all the fullness should dwell" (verse 19). Jesus was the *begotten* Son of God. He was a perfect reflection of God's nature from the moment of His birth. We are the *born-again, in-the-process-of-becoming-perfect* children of God. From the moment of our spiritual rebirth, the Holy Spirit indwells us and begins to grow us to reflect Christ's nature.

Our future *is* that we will be like Christ. We will be perfect, whole, complete—just as He is perfect, whole, and complete. God's plan for our lives is to lead us into that perfection, wholeness, completion, and fullness. As Jesus said, "You shall be perfect, just as your Father in heaven is perfect" (Matthew 5:48). Paul added, "He who has begun a good work in you will complete it until the day of Jesus Christ" (Philippians 1:6), and, "All Scripture is given by inspiration of God, and is profitable for doctrine . . . that the man of God may be complete, thoroughly equipped for every good work" (2 Timothy 3:16–17).

As the author of Hebrews prayed, "Now may the God of peace who brought up our Lord Jesus from the dead, that great Shepherd of the sheep, through the blood of the everlasting covenant, make you complete in every good work to do His will, working in you what is well pleasing in His sight, through Jesus Christ, to whom be glory forever and ever" (13:20–21). Notice in each of these verses the theme of God bringing us to a perfect reflection of Himself.

What a glorious future lies ahead for us! It is *God* who does the sanctifying, cleansing, and perfecting work in us—by His Word and by His presence. He is the One who makes us whole. Our perfection is not something that we can achieve or should strive to achieve. Our perfection is not of our own doing. We are *His* workmanship.

1. "Now by this we know that we are in Him, if we keep His commandments. He who says, 'I know Him,' and does not keep His commandments, is a liar, and the truth is not in him. But whoever keeps His word, truly the love of God is perfected in him. By this we know that we are in Him" (1 John 2:3–5). How is God's love perfected in you?

....

....

....

....

....

....

....

2. What is God's part in making you complete? What is your part?

....
....
....
....
....
....
....
....
....
....
....

PARTICIPATE IN THE PERFECTING PROCESS

The process of our perfection may be painful at times. When artists seek to create a great work—a masterpiece—they must chisel the stone, sand the wood, and refine and pour the metal. In the same way, God will often bring us into difficult situations so we can deepen our reliance on Him and grow in our relationship with Him. We are like clay in His hands.

God described this process to the prophet Jeremiah: "The word which came to Jeremiah from the LORD, saying: 'Arise and go down to the potter's house, and there I will cause you to hear My words.' Then I went down to the potter's house, and there he was, making something at the wheel. And the vessel that he made of clay was marred in the hand of the potter; so he made it again into another vessel, as it seemed good to the potter to make. Then the word of the LORD came to me, saying: 'O house of Israel, can I not do with you as this potter?' says the LORD. 'Look, as the clay is in the potter's hand, so are you in My hand'" (Jeremiah 18:1–6).

Often, God's perfecting of us will also involve a cleansing process. As the prophet Malachi wrote, "He will sit as a refiner and a purifier of silver; He will purify the sons of Levi, and purge them as gold and silver, that they may offer to the LORD an offering in righteousness" (3:3). When I visit some of the famous art galleries and museums in the world, I like to look for my favorite paintings. In one museum, I noticed a particular piece was missing. I asked a guide if it had been sold to another museum. He responded, "No, it is just out being cleaned."

From time to time, God likewise will need to remove us from the spotlight so He can cleanse something from our lives. His perfecting work is to remove impurities so we might better reflect His perfect nature. As Peter wrote, "In this you greatly rejoice, though now for a little while, if need be, you have been grieved by various trials, that the genuineness of your faith, being much more precious than gold that perishes, though it is tested by fire, may be found to praise, honor, and glory at the revelation of Jesus Christ" (1 Peter 1:6–7).

3. "As the clay is in the potter's hand, so are you in My hand" (Jeremiah 18:6). When have you felt that the Lord was remaking you on His potter's wheel?

4. "Behold, I have refined you, but not as silver; I have tested you in the furnace of affliction" (Isaiah 48:10). Silver is refined with hot flames in a furnace. What does this suggest about God's process of purifying His children?

....

....

....

....

....

....

....

....

....

....

LIVE WITH A FORGIVEN IDENTITY

As we participate with God in the refining process, we must remember that just as we have been forgiven, so we are called to forgive ourselves. Forgiving others is a *commandment*. Jesus said, "Forgive, and you will be forgiven" (Luke 6:37), and, "Forgive . . . that your Father in heaven may also forgive you your trespasses. But if you do not forgive, neither will your Father in heaven forgive your trespasses" (Mark 11:25–26). We have received forgiveness freely from the Lord . . . and we are to freely extend that same forgiveness to others.

Furthermore, we are never to keep the good news of God's forgiveness to ourselves. Just as an artist creates a masterpiece for the world to see, so He desires for us to use every opportunity to tell others about His love and salvation. In forgiving others, we give witness to God's desire to forgive. But we must go beyond the example of our lives to actually telling others that God loves them and how they can receive God's forgiveness.

Finally, we are to live as forgiven saints, walking boldly into the life that God has for us. This means true repentance—responding to God's refining process by turning from all things we know are displeasing to Him and choosing to obey His commandments. Our identity is no longer associated with darkness, evil, guilt, shame, or death. Rather, our identity is linked to light, goodness, love, joy, and eternal life. We are to walk truly as children of the light!

5. "For if you forgive men their trespasses, your heavenly Father will also forgive you. But if you do not forgive men their trespasses, neither will your Father forgive your trespasses" (Matthew 6:14–15). Why is it vitally important that we forgive others?

6. "He said to them, 'Go into all the world and preach the gospel to every creature'" (Mark 16:15). Where does Jesus command you to preach? What kinds of people does He ask you to reach with the gospel? How are you seeking to obey this command?

7. "If we say that we have fellowship with Him, and walk in darkness, we lie and do not practice the truth. But if we walk in the light as He is in the light, we have fellowship with one another, and the blood of Jesus Christ His Son cleanses us from all sin" (1 John 1:6–7). What does it mean to "walk in darkness"? What does it mean to "practice the truth"? Why does walking in God's truth need "practice"?

BELIEVING GOD FOR PERFECTION

God alone does the work of perfecting us—of making us, remaking us, refining us. So what is our part? Our part is simply to *receive by faith what God is doing in our lives.* We are to take God at His Word and trust Him to do His work in us. We are to open ourselves to His work, invite Him to do His work in us, and believe that He is at work even when we can't see the results.

God is always behind the scenes of our lives, turning all things toward an eternal benefit for us. Remember Paul's words: "In Him also we have obtained an inheritance, being predestined according to the purpose of Him who works all things according to the counsel of His will" (Ephesians 1:11). We are God's workmanship. He never removes His grace from our lives. He never withdraws or takes His hand off of us. We are always in His everlasting arms . . . and He is always working according to His will. What God begins, He will complete.

It is God who says that the moment you received Jesus Christ as your Savior, you were *in Christ.* It is God who says that He chose you, loves you, has redeemed you from the bondage of sin, and has forgiven you and changed your sin nature. It is God who declares that you are His heir, an enlightened saint with the mind of Christ, a member of the body of Christ, and a holy vessel in His hands. It is God who declares that you are His masterpiece.

The real question facing you today is this: *Will you believe what God says about you?* Will you take Him at His word, by faith, and trust Him to do His work in you?

8. "Trust in the LORD with all your heart, and lean not on your own understanding; In all your ways acknowledge Him, and He shall direct your paths" (Proverbs 3:5–6). When are times you have leaned on your own understanding? What were the results?

9. "Let us lay aside every weight, and the sin which so easily ensnares us, and let us run with endurance the race that is set before us" (Hebrews 12:1). What race has been set for you this week? What sort of endurance is the Lord asking of you?

10. "[Look] unto Jesus, the author and finisher of our faith, who for the joy that was set before Him endured the cross, despising the shame, and has sat down at the right hand of the throne of God" (Hebrews 12:2). What motivated Jesus to go to the cross? How can you find that same motivation in "running the race" for Christ?

TODAY AND TOMORROW

Today: God is at work in my life, refining me and shaping me into a perfect reflection of His Son.

Tomorrow: I will follow God's leading as He does this purifying and perfecting work in my life.

CLOSING PRAYER

Heavenly Father, convict us today to respond to the truth in Your Word that we are Your masterpieces. We have been created to do good works for You in Christ Jesus. Motivate us to act on that truth today. Show us what we can do to get moving and get busy to accomplish the work that You have for us to do. Direct us in ways that we can serve others and share the message of salvation to a lost and hopeless world. Put us to work in Your kingdom. Thank You for the identity we have been given in Christ. Help us to walk worthy today of that high calling.

NOTES AND
PRAYER REQUESTS

Use this space to write any key points, questions, or prayer requests from this week's study.

LEADER'S GUIDE

Thank you for choosing to lead your group through this Bible study from Dr. Charles F. Stanley on *Discovering Your Identity*. The rewards of being a leader are different from those of participating, and it is our prayer that your own walk with Jesus will be deepened by this experience. During the twelve lessons in this study, you will be helping your group members explore and discuss key themes about how they can discover and live out their identity as followers of Christ. There are multiple components in this section that can help you structure your lessons and discussion time, so please be sure to read and consider each one.

BEFORE YOU BEGIN

Before your first meeting, make sure your group members each have a copy of *Discovering Your Identity* so they can follow along in the study guide and have their answers written out ahead of time. Alternately, you can hand out the study guides at your first meeting and give the group members some time to look over the material and ask any preliminary questions. During your first meeting, be sure to send a sheet around the room and have the members write down their name, phone number, and email address so you can keep in touch with them during the week.

To ensure everyone has a chance to participate in the discussion, the ideal size for a group is around eight to ten people. If there are more than ten people, break up the bigger group into smaller sub-groups. Make sure the members are committed to participating each week, as this will help create stability and help you better prepare the structure of the meeting.

At the beginning of each meeting, you may wish to start the group time by asking the group members to provide their initial reactions to the material they have read during the week. The goal is to just get the group members' preliminary thoughts—so encourage them at this point to keep their answers brief. Ideally, you want everyone in the group to get a chance to share some of their thoughts, so try to keep the responses to a minute or less.

Give the group members a chance to answer, but tell them to feel free to pass if they wish. With the rest of the study, it's generally not a good idea to have everyone answer every question—a free-flowing discussion is more desirable. But with the opening icebreaker questions, you can go around the circle. Encourage shy people to share, but don't force them. Also, try to keep any one person from dominating the discussion so everyone will have the opportunity to participate.

WEEKLY PREPARATION

As the group leader, there are a few things you can do to prepare for each meeting:

- *Be thoroughly familiar with the material in the lesson.* Make sure you understand the content of each lesson so you know how to structure the group time and are prepared to lead the group discussion.

- *Decide, ahead of time, which questions you want to discuss.* Depending on how much time you have each week, you may not be able to reflect on every question. Select specific questions that you feel will evoke the best discussion.

- *Take prayer requests.* At the end of your discussion, take prayer requests from your group members and then pray for one another.

- *Pray for your group.* Pray for your group members throughout the week and ask God to lead them as they study His Word.

- *Bring extra supplies to your meeting.* The members should bring their own pens for writing notes, but it's a good idea to have extras available for those who forget. You may also want to bring paper and additional Bibles.

STRUCTURING THE GROUP DISCUSSION TIME

You will need to determine with your group how long you want to meet each week so you can plan your time accordingly. Generally, most groups like to meet for either sixty minutes or ninety minutes, so you could use one of the following schedules:

SECTION	60 Minutes	90 Minutes
WELCOME (group members arrive and get settled)	5 minutes	10 minutes
ICEBREAKER (group members share their initial thoughts regarding the content in the lesson)	10 minutes	15 minutes
DISCUSSION (discuss the Bible study questions you selected ahead of time)	35 minutes	50 minutes
PRAYER/CLOSING (pray together as a group and dismiss)	10 minutes	15 minutes

As the group leader, it is up to you to keep track of the time and keep things moving according to your schedule. If your group is having a good discussion, don't feel the need to stop and move on to the next question. Remember, the purpose is to pull together ideas and share unique insights on the lesson. Encourage everyone to participate, but don't be concerned if certain group members are more quiet. They may just be internally reflecting on the questions and need time to process their ideas before they can share them.

Group Dynamics

Leading a group study can be a rewarding experience for you and your group members—but that doesn't mean there won't be challenges. Certain members may feel uncomfortable in discussing topics that they consider very personal and might be afraid of being called on. Some members might have disagreements on specific issues. To help prevent these scenarios, consider establishing the following ground rules:

- If someone has a question that may seem off topic, suggest that it is discussed at another time, or ask the group if they are okay with addressing that topic.

- If someone asks a question to which you do not know the answer, confess that you don't know and move on. If you feel comfortable, you can invite the other group members to give their opinions or share their comments based on personal experience.

- If you feel like a couple of people are talking much more than others, direct questions to people who may not have shared yet. You could even ask the more dominating members to help draw out the quiet ones.

152

- When there is a disagreement, encourage the members to process the matter in love. Invite members from opposing sides to evaluate their opinions and consider the ideas of the other members. Lead the group through Scripture that addresses the topic, and look for common ground.

When issues arise, encourage your group to follow these words from Scripture: "Love one another" (John 13:34), "If it is possible, as much as depends on you, live peaceably with all men" (Romans 12:18), "Whatever things are true . . . noble . . . pure . . . lovely . . . if there is any virtue and if there is anything praiseworthy—meditate on these things" (Philippians 4:8), and "Be swift to hear, slow to speak, slow to wrath" (James 1:19). This will make your group time more rewarding and beneficial for everyone who attends.

Thank you again for your willingness to lead your group. May God reward your efforts and dedication, equip you to guide your group in the weeks ahead, and make your time together in *Discovering Your Identity* fruitful for His kingdom.

Also Available from Charles F. Stanley

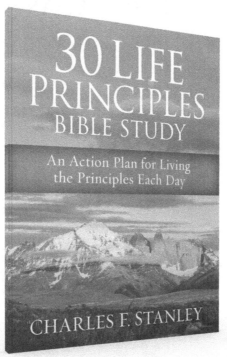

9780310082521   Softcover

30 LIFE PRINCIPLES BIBLE STUDY
An Action Plan for Living the Principles Each Day

During his many years of ministry, Dr. Charles Stanley has faithfully highlighted the 30 life principles that have guided him and helped him to grow in his knowledge, service, and love of God. In this Bible study, you will explore each of these principles in depth and learn how to make them a part of your everyday life. As you do, you will find yourself growing in your relationship with Christ and on the road to the future God has planned for you.

Available now at your favorite bookstore.

Also Available in the
CHARLES F. STANLEY
Bible Study Series

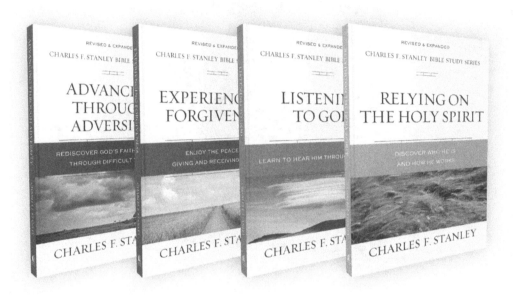

Each study draws on Dr. Stanley's many years of teaching the guiding principles found in God's Word, showing how we can apply them in practical ways to every situation we face. This edition of the series has been completely revised and updated, and includes two brand-new lessons from Dr. Stanley.

Available now at your favorite bookstore.
More volumes coming soon.

The Charles F. Stanley Bible Study Series is a unique approach to Bible study, incorporating biblical truth, personal insights, emotional responses, and a call to action.

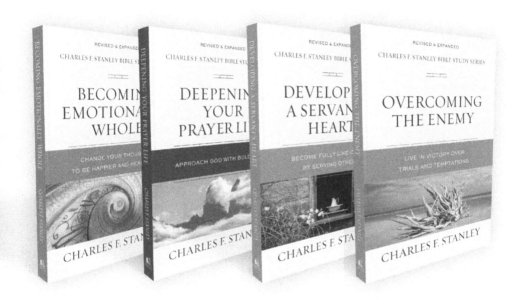

THOMAS NELSON
Since 1798

Printed in the USA
CPSIA information can be obtained
at www.ICGtesting.com
JSHW011407220424
61653JS00009B/91